Essential Spanish Grammar in Review

Essential Spanish
Grammar in Review

Essential Spanish Grammar in Review

John Koppenhaver • Lynn Winget

Wichita State University

McGraw-Hill, Inc.
New York St. Louis San Francisco Auckland Bogotá
Caracas Lisbon London Madrid Mexico City Milan
Montreal New Delhi San Juan Singapore
Sydney Tokyo Toronto

ESSENTIAL SPANISH GRAMMAR IN REVIEW

First Edition

Printed and bound by Book-mart Press, Inc.

10 11 12 13 14 15 16 17 18 19 20 21 BKMBKM 9 9 8 7 6 5

Library of Congress Cataloging in Publication Data

Koppenhaver, John H., 1941–
   Essential Spanish grammar in review.

   English and Spanish.
   Includes index.
   1. Spanish language—Grammar—1950–
1. Winget, Lynn W. II. Title
PC4112.K65   1982   868.2′421   82-18072
ISBN 0-07-554451-2

Text and cover design by Jean LoGrasso and John Reuter-Pacyna

Cover photo by YAN

Preface

Essential Spanish Grammar in Review is intended for use in any situation in which the basic grammatical concepts of Spanish are to be reviewed. This text is designed for maximum flexibility; the eighteen chapters are treated as self-contained units, each concentrating on a particular point of grammar or area of usage. Thus, all of the chapters or only some of them may be used in any given course, in any order the instructor chooses. This flexibility means that the book can be used as the sole text in a course devoted exclusively to grammar review or as a supplement in other courses.

In the grammatical explanations (especially in the chapters dealing with the areas that give English speakers the most trouble, such as **ser** and **estar** or the subjunctive), we have tried, without in any way slighting the specific details of how the particular verb tenses or vocabulary items are used, to give the student a feel for the general principles of the point under discussion, a kind of "general theory" of the preterit and the imperfect or of **por** and **para**.

We believe that there is really no substitute for a great abundance of exercises, and the exercise section of each chapter contains fifty to a hundred items. These are distributed among a wide variety of types of exercises: substitution, transformation, completion, question and answer, and translation from English to Spanish. After the more "structured" exercises, most chapters end with a suggestion for an original composition, usually with a passage in Spanish provided as a model.

Essential Spanish Grammar in Review was originally designed as the text for a course in the authors' department described as "advanced grammar and composition." This course is usually taken by students in their fourth or fifth semester of college Spanish. Subsequent revision and expansion, however, has resulted in a text which can be used in a wide range of courses devoted partly or completely to grammar review and composition.

Because the explanations are presented in a "conversational" style of English, it is assumed that students will not have serious difficulty with them. Therefore, little or no actual classroom time is devoted to the explanation portion of each chapter. All exercises may be done orally in class, although only some of them are so labeled. As this material has been used by the authors over a period of several years, the classroom has become a "seminar" on each grammatical point discussed. Different students present their answers to the various exercises and challenge or correct each other. This procedure allows the class to be conducted entirely in Spanish and requires active participation by all students while minimizing the role of the teacher who must step in only when the group cannot reach a decision as to how to handle a particular construction.

A set of self-checking exercises for each chapter is included after Chapter 18, with answers provided in Appendix A. Appendices B, C, and D include useful sections on numbers, days, months, and seasons; a personal pronouns table; and charts for regular, irregular, and stem-changing verbs.

To facilitate the role of the instructor, we have prepared an instructor's manual (available from McGraw-Hill, Inc.) which contains suggested responses for most exercises in the text.

We want to express our thanks to the students and colleagues who used these materials in their preliminary form. For their helpful comments and suggestions we are very appreciative. Our thanks also go to Karen Koppenhaver and Joan Bergkamp for the excellent typing of the manuscript.

For their constructive criticism of the text we wish to express our appreciation to: Armando Armengol, University of Texas at El Paso; E. Dale Carter, Jr., California State University—Los Angeles; Mary Gay Doman, University of California—Santa Barbara; Gilda Alvarez Evans, University of Texas at Arlington; J. Ray Green, University of Wisconsin—Milwaukee; Elizabeth T. Howe, Tufts University; Coleman Jeffers, University of Iowa; Joan M. Knight, California Polytechnic State University—San Luis Obispo; Martha Marks, Northwestern University; Douglas Morgenstern, Massachusetts Institute of Technology; Luis Pinto, City University of New York Bronx Community College; Franklin Waltman, State University College at Cortland.

We are also indebted to Michael Anderson, Christine Silvestri, Linda Peterson, and Susan Strunk of Scott, Foresman and Company for their guidance and patience in the preparation of the final version of the book.

John Koppenhaver

Lynn Winget

Contents

Essential Spanish Grammar in Review

Essential Spanish
Grammar in Review

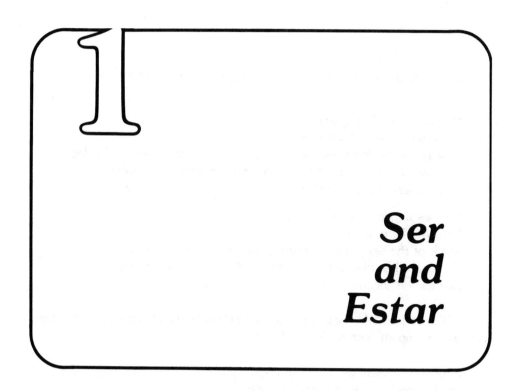

Ser and Estar

Spanish has two verbs meaning *to be:* **ser** (from Latin *esse,* 'to be,' plus a few forms derived from *sedere,* 'to sit') and **estar** (from Latin *stare,* 'to stand'). To differentiate the two verbs correctly, it is useful to keep the following points in mind.

1. Where something is, its location, is virtually always expressed by **estar**.

Argel **está** en Argelia.
Algiers is in Algeria.

Pánfila **estaba** en la cocina.
Pánfila was in the kitchen.

Note the following usages, which sometimes bother English speakers or seem to them to be exceptions to the **estar**-for-location rule.

El baile **será** en el Hotel Urdiñola.
The dance will be at the Urdiñola Hotel.
(Use **ser** in talking about where an event takes place or an activity

is carried on, rather than the physical location of an actual object or person.)

Mi cuñada **es** de Córcega.
My sister-in-law is from Corsica.
(Use **ser** in talking about where a person is from. After all, the fact that my sister-in-law is from Corsica tells us absolutely nothing about where she is, about her location.)

Aquí **es** donde vivimos.
Here is where we live.
Think of the sentence as meaning that this place is the place where we live, rather than that some actual thing—our house, for example—is located here.

2. When a form of *to be* is completed by a noun (or something used like a noun, such as a pronoun), **ser** is almost always used.

El doctor Villegas **es** un buen amigo mío.
Dr. Villegas is a good friend of mine.
(**Amigo** is a noun.)

Echegaray **fue** un famoso dramaturgo español.
Echegaray was a famous Spanish playwright.
(**Dramaturgo** is a noun.)

¿Quién **es**? **Soy** yo.
Who is it? It's me.
(**Quién** and **yo** are pronouns.)

3. When a form of *to be* is completed by an adjective, **ser** is used if the adjective expresses a characteristic that is more or less inherent in the thing or person being discussed, something that is part of what the thing or person is actually like, something that tells what kind of a thing or person it is (at least in the opinion of the speaker).

El japonés **es** difícil.
Japanese is difficult.
(What kind of a language is Japanese? It's a difficult language.)

El tabaco no **es** bueno para la salud.
Tobacco isn't good for one's health.
(What is the nature of tobacco? What is it like? It's not good for your health.)

Raúl es joven, rico, inteligente y bien parecido.
Raúl is young, rich, intelligent, and good looking.
(What is Raúl like? He's young, rich, intelligent, and good looking.)

Although "impersonal" expressions could probably be shown without too much difficulty to fit the rule just stated, it may be more useful for practical purposes to regard the various impersonal expressions, almost all of which use **ser**, as a special category: **es cierto** *(it is true)*, **es posible** *(it is possible)*, **es importante** *(it is important)*, **es preciso** *(it is necessary)*, **es evidente** *(it is obvious)*, **es peligroso** *(it is dangerous)*, **es probable** *(it is probable)*, etc. Note, however, **está bien** *(it is all right)*.

4. When a form of *to be* is completed by an adjective, **estar** is used if the adjective refers to a state or condition rather than an inherent characteristic.

El café **está** frío.
The coffee is cold.
(Being cold is the state the coffee happens to be in. It is not in the nature of coffee to be either hot or cold.)

No **estoy** triste. Tampoco **estoy** enojado. **Estoy** cansado nada más.
I'm not sad. I'm not angry either. I'm just tired.
(Being sad, angry, and tired are all states or conditions. They do not refer to the kind of person I am, to what I am really like.)

El baño de esa casa siempre **está** sucio.
The bathroom in that house is always dirty.
(A dirty bathroom is not a particular type or kind of bathroom. Being dirty is simply a condition bathrooms sometimes get into.)

5. A few adjectives, in accordance with the principles just stated, have rather specific, well-defined meanings depending on whether they are used with **ser** or **estar**: **ser listo** *(to be smart, intelligent)* but **estar listo** *(to be ready);* **ser aburrido** *(to be boring)* but **estar aburrido** *(to be bored);* **ser cansado** *(to be tiresome)* but **estar cansado** *(to be tired);* **ser malo** *(to be bad)* but (in many parts of the Spanish-speaking world) **estar malo** *(to be sick).*

6. **Estar** plus an adjective is often used even in talking about what might seem to be inherent characteristics, if the speaker's intention is to comment on his reaction to something he has experienced.

Me gusta la paella. **Es** muy buena.
I like paella. It's very good.

But: Me gusta esta paella. **Está** muy buena.
I like this paella. It's very good.
(This paella I am actually engaged in eating tastes good to me.)

Me han dicho que tu casa **es** muy bonita.
I have been told your house is very pretty.

But: ¡Qué bonita **está** tu casa!
How pretty your house is!
(Your house, which I am now seeing for myself, looks very pretty to me.)

Los terremotos a veces **son** muy fuertes.
Earthquakes sometimes are very severe.

But: El terremoto de la semana pasada **estuvo** muy fuerte.
The earthquake last week (which I was in) was very severe.
(It is not my intention here to make an abstract statement about the nature of earthquakes but to comment on my reaction to a particular one I actually experienced.)

7. **Estar** plus an adjective is often used to comment on a change or a contrast with what the speaker had regarded as normal.

El azafrán **es** muy caro.
Saffron is very expensive.
(It's the nature of saffron to be expensive.)

But: El azafrán **está** muy caro.
Saffron is very expensive (now).
(It's more expensive than usual. The price has recently gone up.)

Amalia **es** muy flaca.
Amalia is very thin.
(It's normal for her to be thin. That's the kind of person she is.)

But: Amalia **está** muy flaca.
Amalia is very thin.
(She's looking unusually thin. She's lost weight.)

8. Used with the past participle of a verb, **ser** generally refers to an event or action; **estar** refers to the situation that exists when the action is over.

A las nueve las puertas **fueron abiertas.**
At nine o'clock the doors were opened.

(The act of opening the doors occurred at nine o'clock. At nine o'clock somebody came and opened the doors.)

A las nueve las puertas ya **estaban abiertas.**
At nine o'clock the doors were already open.
(The act of opening the doors had occurred earlier and was already over.)

El general **fue herido** en la batalla.
The general was wounded (got wounded) in the battle.
(The wounding of the general—the event, the act—occurred in the battle.)

Vi que el general **estaba herido.**
I saw that the general was wounded.
(The event had already happened and was over.)

Combinations of **ser** and a past participle (such as the **fueron abiertas** and the **fue herido** of the preceding examples) are referred to as the *passive voice* and are usually thought of as part of the conjugation of the verb in question. This so-called true passive is not used as much in Spanish as it is in English. (Constructions that can replace the passive are discussed in Chapter 12.)

Not all examples, or apparent examples, of **ser** or **estar** used with a past participle fit the above rule. Some words that look like past participles and perhaps originally were, such as **honrado** *(honest)* or **divertido** *(amusing),* are simply adjectives and as such are used with **ser** or **estar** according to the same principles that apply to any other adjective. Some English-speakers may also have trouble with examples like **estar equivocado** *(to be mistaken)* and **estar enamorado** *(to be in love).* Though in a very broad sense, these examples *do* represent the situation that exists after an action or event has taken place in much the same way that **estar herido** does. (Somebody wounded me, and now, as a result, I am wounded. I made a wrong judgment or formed a wrong opinion, and now, as a result, I am mistaken. I fell in love, and now, as a result, I am in love.)

9. **Estar** (never **ser**) combines with **-ndo** verb forms to produce *progressive* constructions—so called because they refer to something that is "in progress."

Estaba lloviendo.
It was raining.

Están trabajando.
They're working.

In Spanish, unlike English, these constructions cannot be used to report things planned for the future. Therefore, use the simple present or future tense, not the present progressive, when referring to the future.

Salimos (*or* **saldremos**) mañana.
We are leaving tomorrow.

In addition, progressive constructions traditionally have not been used with verbs of motion as much as they are in English (possibly because **estar** comes from a word that meant *to stand*, and it would be contradictory to suggest that a person was standing still and moving at the same time). Therefore, do not use the progressive tenses with verbs of motion.

¿Adónde **vas**?
Where are you going?

Venía del mercado.
I was coming from the market.

• EXERCISE A

Complete the following sentences using **ser** or **estar** in the tense indicated.

1. El señor _____ chileno, pero _____ radicado *(located)* en Barcelona. (past)
2. Usted _____ equivocado, María _____ la más linda. (present)
3. _____ hora de que ellos _____ aquí. (present)
4. El pobre _____ cada día más loco. (past)
5. La fiesta _____ en la casa de Juan. (future)
6. _____ bien que lo digas, pero _____ seguro que no te creerán. (present)
7. _____ cierto que Ricardo _____ mayor, pero Jorge _____ más alto con esos zapatos. (past)
8. Aunque _____ un hombre muy fuerte, parece _____ algo enfermo hoy. (present)
9. _____ preciosa con ese vestido azul. (past)
10. _____ que no quería _____ allí para la Navidad. (present)
11. La ciudad _____ sometida a un incesante bombardeo. (past)
12. Tú _____ en lo cierto, _____ amarillo, no anaranjado. (past)
13. Ese trabajo _____ terminado, así que déjalo donde _____ . (present)
14. Con lo inteligente que _____ Mario, me sorprende lo equivocado que _____ . (present)
15. Si el dinero que ha ganado _____ mucho, _____ preciso pagar más impuestos. (present—future)

• EXERCISE B

Express a logical conclusion to the sentence given using **ser** or **estar** in a new sentence.

Example:
El Sr. Rodríguez enseña en la universidad.
El Sr. Rodríguez **es** profesor.

Cuando salí de casa llovía mucho.
Estoy mojado.

1. Me gusta mucho la sopa.
2. La sopa tiene muchas legumbres.
3. Encontré que no había nadie en la casa.
4. Hay gran distancia de aquí a Buenos Aires.
5. Usaron ladrillos para construir el edificio nuevo.
6. Jorge nació en Guadalajara.
7. María Elena acaba de correr tres millas y no da más.
8. Tengo fiebre y me duele todo el cuerpo.
9. No creo que quieras ese café ya que te lo sirvieron hace veinte minutos.
10. Roberto apagó todas las luces y no veo nada.

• EXERCISE C

Complete the following sentences using **ser** or **estar** in the tense indicated.

1. _____ un hermoso animal, pero ten cuidado que no _____ completamente domesticado. (present)
2. Esa novela _____ de Camilo José Cela, la escribió mientras _____ en Madrid. (present—past)
3. _____ de suponer que _____ lista para mañana. (present—future)
4. Me _____ difícil creer que _____ tan sucia cuando ella _____ una persona tan pulcra (tidy). (past)
5. Rosa _____ lista, pero no _____ bien preparada para el examen. (present—past)
6. Me dijeron que la reunión _____ en el club, pero cuando llegué no _____ ninguno de ellos. (past)
7. _____ elegido director del comité. (past)
8. _____ de acuerdo. Vas a _____ muy ocupado desde ahora en adelante. (present)

9. _____ muy mal decir eso delante de su mamá. (past)
10. ¡No te vayas a quemar, el café _____ muy caliente! (present)
11. _____ las cuatro de la mañana cuando anunciaron que _____ dispuestos a aceptar el trato. (past)
12. El candidato _____ apoyado por la mayoría del pueblo. (past)
13. Generalmente no me gusta la comida que preparan allí, pero hoy _____ riquísima. (past)
14. Sus amigos _____ los que no dijeron nada. (present)
15. Mañana _____ cuando se lo daré. (present)
16. _____ contenta de que ahora _____ suya. (present)
17. Ella _____ soltera, su hermano _____ el que _____ casado. (past)
18. Por favor, tráigame otro, este saco me _____ muy chico. (present)
19. Yo _____ muy alegre anoche en la fiesta. Tenía que _____ por el vino. (past)
20. Perdóname, no puedo hablar contigo ahora, _____ tarde y _____ muy apurado. (present)
21. ¿_____ rico? No, ponle más azúcar, por favor. (present)
22. Esa manzana _____ verde (unripe). No la comas, que te vas a enfermar. (present)
23. Esta conversación _____ muy interesante, pero _____ muy cansado ahora. (present)
24. _____ bien que no quieras _____ presente, pero _____ bien educado y díselo. (present)
25. _____ un día hermoso. El cielo _____ completamente despejado (clear), y además _____ enamorado otra vez. (past)

• EXERCISE D

Translate the following sentences into Spanish.

1. The truth is that I have never been in such a place.
2. I'm bored with this lesson. When are we going to be ready for the next one?
3. He seems to be very comfortable in that chair of yours.
4. It's seven o'clock. That is the time that you were supposed to be ready.
5. It has been raining a lot this spring, so the gardens are going to be beautiful.
6. If you had been in class yesterday, you would understand what he is saying.
7. The life they led there was very easy. Why do they always have to be moving?
8. You ought to be more courteous when speaking to her. She is your mother.
9. The cafeteria is where I'm asking you to be.
10. The president was assassinated by a group of terrorists.
11. I'm of the opinion that you are wrong. Please, be quiet!

12. The sweater may be wool, but it is not handmade.
13. No matter how many times I clean it, this house is always dirty.
14. Don't be dumb! If you are tired, go to bed.
15. Be still! When I'm ready to see you, I'll call you.

• EXERCISE E

In all of the following sentences **ser** plus a past participle is used to report an action or event (the "true passive"). For each sentence make up a corresponding sentence in which you use **estar** plus a past participle to describe the resulting situation or state. You may add, delete, or modify other elements in the sentence if you want to and it seems appropriate to do so.

Example:
Las puertas del palacio **habían sido abiertas** a primera hora de la mañana.
Cuando nosotros llegamos al palacio, las puertas ya **estaban abiertas**.

1. Estoy seguro de que el trabajo habrá sido terminado antes de que tú llegues.
2. La carta fue escrita en árabe por el secretario del embajador.
3. Según tengo entendido, todas esas ventanas fueron rotas hace varias semanas.
4. Dicen que la Galia había sido dividida en tres partes mucho antes de la llegada de los romanos.
5. Por fin han sido convencidos de lo poco convenientes que son sus sugerencias.
6. No sabía que el dictador había sido asesinado por los insurgentes.
7. La capital fue destruida casi totalmente durante la guerra.
8. La universidad fue cerrada por el gobierno hace mucho tiempo.
9. Espero que los platos ya hayan sido lavados.
10. ¿Para cuándo crees que habrá sido publicada esa novela?

• EXERCISE F

Answer the following questions with complete Spanish sentences, or at least sentences complete enough to contain a conjugated verb.

1. ¿De dónde es Ud. y de dónde son sus padres?
2. ¿De quién y de qué es la casa o el apartamento donde vive Ud. ahora?

3. ¿Dónde está Ud. ahora y por o para qué?
4. ¿Cómo es Ud.?
5. Si pudiera estar Ud. en cualquier parte del mundo, ¿dónde le gustaría estar y por qué?
6. ¿Cómo es la ciudad donde vive Ud?
7. ¿Cuáles son algunas frutas que pueden ser verdes aunque no estén verdes (unripe)?
8. ¿Cree Ud. que todos los que están en los manicomios son locos de verdad?
9. Si no están locos, ¿por qué están en el manicomio?
10. ¿Conoce Ud. a alguien que a pesar de ser muy viejo no esté muy viejo?
11. ¿Sabe Ud. de qué país eran sus bisabuelos?
12. ¿Sabe Ud. cómo era ese país?
13. ¿Es posible no ser feliz y sin embargo estar contento?
14. ¿De qué autor es su novela predilecta (favorite)?
15. ¿En qué idioma está escrita?

• EXERCISE G

Write a one-page true or fictional autobiography. Be sure to include your ancestors, where they came from, where they have been, and what they were like. In the paragraphs about yourself describe your physical traits as well as mental attitudes. Be imaginative! See how many different uses of **ser** and **estar** you can correctly incorporate.

"Yo soy . . . "

Stem-changing Verbs

Spanish verb forms are sometimes described as consisting of a "stem" and an "ending." According to this terminology, the stem of a verb form like **hablo** is **habl-**, and the ending is **-o**; the stem of **escribe** is **escrib-**, and the ending is **-e**; the stem of **comió** is **com-**, and the ending is **-ió**.

A number of Spanish verbs do not have the same vowel or diphthong in the stems of all of their forms: p**e**nsar *but* pi**e**nsan, d**o**rmimos *but* d**u**rmieron, m**o**ría *but* m**u**ere, p**e**diré *but* p**i**do, etc. These verbs are usually called *stem-changing* verbs, or occasionally *radical-changing* verbs. (The stem of a verb can also be called its "root," and the term *radical* means literally "pertaining to the root.")

With the apparent exception of **jugar** (which was originally **jogar** in Old Spanish), only verbs with an **e** or an **o** in the stem of the infinitive can be stem-changing. All **-ir** verbs with an **e** or an **o** in their infinitive stem are stem-changing (the only ones with **o** in common use in modern Spanish are **dormir** and **morir**), but **-ar** and **-er** verbs can be either stem-changing or not: m**o**ver/mu**e**ve *but* c**o**mer/c**o**me, p**e**nsar/pi**e**nsa *but* cond**e**nsar/cond**e**nsa, etc.

In teaching Spanish to English speakers, it is customary to lump together two similar but really quite separate phenomena under the general heading "stem changes." Here we will discuss them separately and will arbitrarily refer to them as Type I and Type II stem changes.

Type I

The only stem changes -ar and -er verbs ever have are of Type I; only -ir verbs have Type II changes also. The "change" here is an alternation between **e** and **ie** (or, in the case of a few -ir verbs, between **e** and **i**) and between **o** and **ue**: sentir/siente, medimos/miden, contáis/cuentas, etc.

In stressed syllables Latin short **e** and short **o** normally became Spanish **ie** and **ue**, but in unstressed syllables this change did not take place. (This is why we have siete *but* setenta or Venezuela *but* venezolano.) What we are here calling Type I stem changes are really nothing but this general principle as it shows up specifically in the Spanish verb system, which means that the presence or absence of these changes is determined completely and without exception by where the stress falls in any given verb form.

The only forms of a Spanish regular verb that are stressed on the stem (rather than the ending) and therefore can have Type I stem changes are the first, second, and third person singular and third person plural of the present indicative and the present subjunctive, and the **tú** affirmative command: muerdo, muerdes, muerde, muerden; muerda, muerdas, muerda, muerdan; ¡muerde! There are never any Type I stem changes in the imperfect, the preterit, the future, the conditional, the past subjunctive, the present participle, the past participle, or the infinitive.

Type II

As mentioned above, only -ir verbs have Type II stem changes. No matter what the Type I stem change of any given verb may be, its Type II change involves an alternation between **e** and **i** or **o** and **u**: servir/sirvieron, dormimos/durmiendo, etc. Unlike Type I changes, Type II changes occur only in unstressed syllables, never in stressed syllables.

Just as the position of the stress is what determines whether a Type I stem change appears in any given verb form, the key to the occurrence of a Type II change is the presence, in the syllable following the stem, of an unstressed **i** plus another vowel; to be more precise, the presence of either **ie** or **io**: sirviendo, murieron, midió, etc. (The first person plural and second person plural of the present subjunctive—for instance, **pidamos** and **pidáis**—are only apparent exceptions, since they come from Latin forms that orginally had an unstressed **i** plus another vowel in the following syllable.)

The specific forms in which Type II stem changes occur are the third person singular and third person plural of the preterit, the first person plural and second person plural of the present subjunctive, all persons and numbers of both of the past subjunctives, and the present participle: murió, murieron; muramos, muráis; muriera, murieras, etc.; muriese, murieses, etc.; muriendo.

As further examples of the various changes, the appropriate tenses of several different stem-changing verbs are given below. For **-ar** and **-er** verbs (Type I stem changes only), **tostar** *(to toast)* and **moler** *(to grind)* exemplify the alternation of **o** with **ue**; **atravesar** *(to cross)* and **defender** *(to defend)* illustrate the alternation of **e** with **ie**. Verbs ending in **-ir** (both Type I and Type II stem changes) are represented by **dormir** *(to sleep)* **(o>ue)**, **divertir** *(to amuse)* **(e>ie)**, and **rendir** *(to render)* **(e>i)**.

Present indicative:

tuesto	muelo	atravieso	defiendo	duermo	divierto	rindo
tuestas	mueles	atraviesas	defiendes	duermes	diviertes	rindes
tuesta	muele	atraviesa	defiende	duerme	divierte	rinde
tostamos	molemos	atravesamos	defendemos	dormimos	divertimos	rendimos
tostáis	moléis	atravesáis	defendéis	dormís	divertís	rendís
tuestan	muelen	atraviesan	defienden	duermen	divierten	rinden

Present subjunctive:

tueste	muela	atraviese	defienda	duerma	divierta	rinda
tuestes	muelas	atravieses	defiendas	duermas	diviertas	rindas
tueste	muela	atraviese	defienda	duerma	divierta	rinda
tostemos	molamos	atravesemos	defendamos	durmamos	divirtamos	rindamos
tostéis	moláis	atraveséis	defendáis	durmáis	divirtáis	rindáis
tuesten	muelan	atraviesen	defiendan	duerman	diviertan	rindan

Imperative:

¡tuesta!	¡muele!	¡atraviesa!	¡defiende!	¡duerme!	¡divierte!	¡rinde!
¡tostad!	¡moled!	¡atravesad!	¡defended!	¡dormid!	¡divertid!	¡rendid!

Preterit:

tosté	molí	atravesé	defendí	dormí	divertí	rendí
tostaste	moliste	atravesaste	defendiste	dormiste	divertiste	rendiste
tostó	molió	atravesó	defendió	durmió	divirtió	rindió
tostamos	molimos	atravesamos	defendimos	dormimos	divertimos	rendimos
tostasteis	molisteis	atravesasteis	defendisteis	dormisteis	divertisteis	rendisteis
tostaron	molieron	atravesaron	defendieron	durmieron	divirtieron	rindieron

Past subjunctive (-ra):

tostara	moliera	atravesara	defendiera	durmiera	divirtiera	rindiera
tostaras	molieras	atravesaras	defendieras	durmieras	divirtieras	rindieras
tostara	moliera	atravesara	defendiera	durmiera	divirtiera	rindiera
tostáramos	moliéramos	atravesáramos	defendiéramos	durmiéramos	divirtiéramos	rindiéramos
tostarais	molierais	atravesarais	defendierais	durmierais	divirtierais	rindierais
tostaran	molieran	atravesaran	defendieran	durmieran	divirtieran	rindieran

Past subjunctive (-se):

tostase	moliese	atravesase	defendiese	durmiese	divirtiese	rindiese
tostases	molieses	atravesases	defendieses	durmieses	divirtieses	rindieses
tostase	moliese	atravesase	defendiese	durmiese	divirtiese	rindiese
tostásemos	moliésemos	atravesásemos	defendiésemos	durmiésemos	divirtiésemos	rindiésemos
tostaseis	molieseis	atravesaseis	defendieseis	durmieseis	divirtieseis	rindieseis
tostasen	moliesen	atravesasen	defendiesen	durmiesen	divirtiesen	rindiesen

Present participle:

tostando	moliendo	atravesando	defendiendo	durmiendo	divirtiendo	rindiendo

• **EXERCISE A**

Change the verbs in the following sentences to make them correspond to the various subjects indicated.

1. ¿A qué hora te acuestas? (ellos, Felipe, ustedes, vosotros)
2. Raúl se arrepintió *(repented)* de haberse casado. (yo, Juana y Pablo, nosotros, tú)
3. Es importante que te sientas orgulloso de tu patria. (yo, vosotros, nosotros, Ana)

4. Me niego a aceptar esas ideas. (el profesor, mi hermana y yo, tú, ellas)
5. Yo me divertí mucho en la fiesta. (esa chica, nosotros, mis primos, tú)
6. Mi hermano mide casi dos metros. (yo, Enrique, tú, nosotros)
7. Siempre se sienta en el mismo rincón. (ustedes, vosotros, Paco y yo, yo)
8. Es preciso que volvamos temprano. (ella, los jóvenes, yo, vosotros)
9. No es probable que durmáis más de siete u ocho horas. (nosotros, tú, el niño, yo)
10. Era imposible que nos despidiésemos de nuestros amigos sin llorar. (él, yo, Rosario, tú)

• EXERCISE B

Complete the following sentences as indicated.

1. _____ (cerrar; Ud.—command) la puerta, _____ (colgar; Ud.—command) su abrigo en esa percha, y _____ (empezar; nosotros—command) a trabajar.
2. No _____ (negar; yo—present) que _____ (pensar; él—present) que siempre _____ (pedir; nosotros—present) lo mismo, pero no es verdad.
3. _____ (sentir; yo—present) mucho que no _____ (preferir; Ud.—present) llegar para la comida.
4. Hoy no me _____ (sentir—present) muy bien. Espero que _____ (repetir; nosotros—present) este ejercicio.
5. Siempre que _____ (perder; ellos—present) un partido de fútbol, se _____ (sentir; ellos—present) muy decaídos por varios días.
6. Yo _____ (servir—future) la sopa si tú _____ (servir—present) el plato fuerte.
7. No me _____ (acordarse—present) si te _____ (decir; yo—past) lo que nos ocurrió anoche. Cuando _____ (volver; tú) te lo digo.
8. Nos dijo que nos _____ (acostar—past) a las once, pero yo no me _____ (acostar—present) hasta estar bien listo.
9. Perro que ladra *(barks)* no _____ (morder—present). Por lo menos así dice el refrán.
10. Este tiempo está insoportable. O _____ (llover—present) o _____ (nevar—present) todos los días.
11. Me parece muy mal que él _____ (sugerir—present) que _____ (mentir; tú—present).
12. _____ (sentir; nosotros—present) mucho que Ud. haya estado _____ (dormir) en vez de prestar atención.
13. _____ (despedirse; nosotros—command) de ellos antes de que se vayan.
14. Nos _____ (pedir; él—past) que no nos _____ (reírse—past) antes de mostrarnos el dibujo.
15. Estaba _____ (medir) el tamaño de la caja fuerte cuando lo sorprendió la policía.

16. Tú _____ (freír—command) los huevos y yo preparo el pan tostado.
17. Da vuelta para acá y _____ (sonreír—present) que vamos a sacar la foto.
18. _____ (medir; tú—command) esa tabla otra vez antes de cortarla.
19. _____ (preferir; yo—present) no hablarle hasta después.
20. ¿ _____ (perder; tú—past) lo que te encargó o no? Si le estás _____ (mentir), va a estar muy disgustado.

• EXERCISE C

Translate the following sentences.

1. Mary wants to sit down because she doesn't feel well.
2. Please don't fall asleep yet. Wait until I return.
3. I don't find it here, and I don't remember where I put it.
4. Remember to put them to bed before I return.
5. Count to ten, then cross the bridge.
6. Close your mouth and bite on this so it won't hurt so much.
7. Show them what she brought you from Paraguay.
8. He will not be able to do it no matter how much you scold him.
9. They prefer not to go until it snows.
10. Don't compete with them when you know that you can't win.

• EXERCISE D

Turn to page 175 and review the list of common stem-changing verbs. Write ten sentences using at least one stem-changing verb in each one.
Be imaginative!

• EXERCISE E

Answer the following questions orally.

1. ¿A qué hora se despierta Ud. los domingos?
2. ¿Duerme Ud. más o menos durante los fines de semana?
3. ¿Durmió bien anoche? ¿Por qué sí o no?
4. ¿Sueña Ud. solamente cuando duerme o también cuando está despierto(a)?
5. ¿Se divierte Ud. cuando juega algún deporte o solamente cuando estudia español?
6. ¿Se acuerda Ud. de algún chiste en español?

7. ¿Piensa Ud. seguir estudiando español el semestre que viene?
8. ¿Prefiere Ud. hablar de la filosofía, la política o la religión?
9. ¿Encuentra Ud. que esta clase es fácil o difícil?
10. ¿Tiene Ud. una persona a quien le cuenta sus pensamientos más íntimos? ¿Quiere decirnos quién es?

• EXERCISE F

Read the following passage carefully. Identify all the stem-changing verbs.

Hay veces en que por más que quiera dormirme, no puedo. Me desvisto y me acuesto como siempre, y sin embargo, siento ya de antemano (in advance) que va a ser una de esas noches. Algunas veces caliento un poco de leche, porque dicen que eso ayuda. Francamente, yo nunca lo encuentro satisfactorio. Como te digo, me acuesto, elijo la posición más cómoda posible, cierro los ojos, y nada. A veces vuelvo a abrir los ojos y concentro la mirada en un punto imaginario en la oscuridad para tratar de adormecerme (get sleepy). Pero nada. Y repito y repito: "¡Tienes que dormirte, estúpido!" Pero no hay caso. Empiezo a pensar, o mejor dicho, sigo pensando en lo que ha ocurrido durante el día, en cualquier bobada, en algún problema no resuelto. Pero lo que quiero es no pensar. Lo divertido es que cuando uno más se esfuerza en dejar de pensar, más difícil es. Y pienso y pienso. Otras veces cuento ovejas. Yo no sé quién inventó eso de contar ovejas. He llegado en ocasiones a cifras increíbles de ovejas y todavía tan despierto. Vuelvo a cerrar los ojos. Los aprieto hasta que me duelen. Sí, ya sé que el dolor no es necesariamente el mejor remedio para el insomnio, pero es que para entonces estoy compitiendo con el sueño. Y me da rabia. Y sigo despierto. Sencillamente no consigo conciliar el sueño.

De repente oigo el despertador que suena como un grillo furioso en la cómoda, y me despierto. No recuerdo cuando me dormí, y me duele un poco la cabeza, pero por lo menos ahora tengo motivo para estar despierto.

Once you have identified all stem-changing verbs, rewrite the passage, but this time change the verbs to the past tense where appropriate.

3

Preterit and Imperfect

We usually speak of the preterit and the imperfect as two *tenses* of the Spanish verb. However, the difference between them is not really a difference in tense. The grammatical term *tense* comes from the Old French word *tens*, which meant 'time,' and in fact several languages simply use an ordinary word for time (for instance, **tiempo** in Spanish) as the technical term for referring to a verb tense. If tense refers to time (past, present, or future), then there is no real difference in tense between the preterit and the imperfect, since both of them refer to the past.

Verbs, however, have another characteristic, generally called *aspect*, which has to do with actions viewed as beginning, continuing, coming to an end, recurring, etc., and the difference between the preterit and the imperfect is really a difference in aspect. In terms of aspect, the following statements can be made about the use of the preterit and the imperfect.

If a particular sentence directs our attention to the *beginning* of whatever the verb expresses (an event, a state of affairs, an activity, a condition), then the preterit is used.

A partir de 1954 **viví** en Cerdeña.
From 1954 on I lived in Sardinia.

(The reference is to the beginning of my stay in Sardinia.)

If a particular sentence directs our attention to the *end* of whatever the verb expresses, then the preterit is used.

Hasta 1961 **viví** en Cerdeña.
Up to 1961 I lived in Sardinia.
(The reference is to the end of my stay in Sardinia.)

If a particular sentence directs our attention to the beginning *and* the end of whatever the verb expresses, then the preterit is used.

De 1954 a 1961 **viví** en Cerdeña.
From 1954 to 1961 I lived in Sardinia.
(The reference is to both the beginning and the end of my stay
in Sardinia.)

If a particular sentence directs our attention to a point at which whatever the verb expresses had already begun but had not yet ended, then the imperfect is used.

Vivía en Cerdeña.
I was living in Sardinia. (I used to live in Sardinia.)
(There is no indication of when I went to Sardinia, how long I stayed,
or when I left; the reference is to a point at which my stay in Sardinia
was already under way and had not yet come to an end.)

In applying this last principle, absolutely all that matters is whether the thing expressed by the verb was still going on *at the time to which the sentence refers;* if it was, then the imperfect is used. When (if ever) the situation or activity may subsequently have come to an end is completely immaterial. English-speaking students of Spanish sometimes try to bring in the question of whether the thing is still in effect *now,* but that is never a factor.

The four principles given above constitute a kind of general theory of the preterit and the imperfect. For the practical application of these principles, the following points are worth noting.

1. For narration the preterit is generally used, since each of the events narrated is seen in its entirety, as something that happened and was over with at that time.

Se levantó, se vistió y bajó al comedor, donde **se comió** una uva.
*He got up, got dressed, and went down to the dining room, where he ate
a grape.*

(The rising, the getting dressed, the descent to the dining room, and the grape-eating are all presented as completed units, each with its beginning and end.)

2. An indication of how long a thing lasted generally calls for a preterit.

Trabajó dos años en una mina de plata.
He worked two years in a silver mine.

3. For description the imperfect is generally used, since there is usually no indication of when the qualities, characteristics, states, or conditions being described came into existence, how long they lasted, or when they came to an end.

Mi primo **era** alto y delgado.
My cousin was tall and slim.
(At that time he had already begun being tall and slim and had not yet ceased to be.)

Era fácil ver que **estaba** enferma.
It was easy to see that she was sick.

But: **Estuvo** enferma tres días.
She was sick three days.
(The mention of how long she was sick reminds us that her illness had a beginning and an end, hence preterit.)

4. English *was* or *were* plus *-ing* generally corresponds to a Spanish imperfect.

Estaba nevando.
It was snowing.
(It had already started snowing and had not yet stopped snowing, hence imperfect.)

5. An actual or implied *used to* (also *would* when it means *used to*) generally corresponds to a Spanish imperfect.

Siempre **usaban** zapatos verdes.
They always wore (always used to wear) green shoes.

Todas las mañanas **íbamos** a la playa.
Every morning we would go (used to go) to the beach.

However, repeated actions appear in the preterit when a definite number of occurrences is mentioned.

Fuimos a la playa cinco veces.
We went to the beach five times.

6. The time of day is always expressed in the imperfect rather than the preterit.

Eran las seis.
It was six o'clock.
(It had already started being 6:00 [after having been 5:59] and had not yet stopped being 6:00 [in order to become 6:01], hence imperfect, although the person who makes such a statement is not usually thinking of it in quite such a hair-splitting way.)

7. What might be called the informative activities of written and printed material are generally talked about in the imperfect.

La carta **decía** que llegarían el viernes.
The letter said they would arrive on Friday.

8. Notice the contrasts illustrated in the following pairs of sentences. Notice also that the preterit and the imperfect of some Spanish verbs are best expressed in English by two different verbs.

Conocí a la señora de Elizondo.
I met Mrs. Elizondo.
(*Met* in the sense of made the acquaintance of, was introduced to. The reference is to the beginning of my acquaintance with Mrs. Elizondo, hence preterit.)

Conocía a la señora de Elizondo.
I knew Mrs. Elizondo.
(The reference is to a point at which my acquaintance with Mrs. Elizondo had already begun and had not yet ended, hence imperfect.)

Supe que eran del País de Gales.
I found out (learned, came to know) that they were from Wales.

Sabía que eran del País de Gales.
I (already) knew that they were from Wales.

Quiso abrir la ventana.
He tried to open the window.
(He conceived a desire to open the window and acted on it; the reference is to the outcome, hence preterit.)

Quería abrir la ventana.
He wanted to open the window.
(The sentence describes his mental attitude with no reference
to its beginning or its end.)

No **pudo** vender el coche.
He didn't succeed in selling the car (didn't manage to sell the car).
(The implication is that he tried to and failed. The reference is to
the outcome.)

No **podía** vender el coche.
He couldn't sell the car.
(The sentence describes a state of affairs, namely, his inability to
sell the car. There is no reference to the outcome.)

Tuvimos que estudiar.
We had to study.
(The implication is that something caused us to have to study and we
did: outcome.)

Teníamos que estudiar.
We had to study.
(The sentence describes a situation in which we had an obligation to
study, but there is no reference to the outcome.)

• EXERCISE A

Complete the following sentences as indicated.

1. Cuando _____ adonde nos _____ , _____ que ya habían salido.
   *When we arrived where they were waiting for us, we found out that they had
   already left.*
2. _____ indicarle que no _____ necesario hacerlo hoy.
   I wanted to tell him that it wasn't necessary to do it today.
3. _____ que _____ a entender lo que Ud. me _____ cuando _____ con eso.
   *I thought I was beginning to understand what you were telling me when you
   came out with that.*
4. _____ hacerle ver que no _____ conveniente, pero no _____
   (form of **hacer caso**).
   I tried to make her see that it wasn't advisable, but she did not pay any attention.
5. Nos _____ que _____ bien, pero no se lo _____ .
   He told us it was all right, but we didn't believe him.

6. Una vez que ____ lo que me ____ , me ____ rotundamente.
   Once I caught on to what they were asking of me, I flatly refused.

7. Apenas ____ el trabajo, lo ____ sin decir palabra.
   The minute he finished the paper, he turned it in without saying a word.

8. Nosotros ____ allí cuando no ____ necesidad de preocuparse con aquello.
   ____ después cuando se ____ fea la cosa.
   We were living there at a time when there was no need to worry about that.
   It was later that things got bad.

9. No me ____ nada, pero ____ ver lo que ____ el cartel.
   They didn't tell me anything, but I managed to see what the sign said.

10. Nos ____ en casa, y mientras ____ , ____ Raimundo y nos ____ que
    todos los arreglos se habían hecho.
    We met at home, and while we were talking, Raimundo arrived and told us
    that all the arrangements had been made.

11. Apenas ____ conciliar el sueño, aunque ____ que le ____ falta.
    He was barely able to get to sleep, even though he knew he needed to.

12. Se ____ (form of **dirigir**) al escritorio donde ____ sus documentos, los
    ____ y se ____ a leerlos lentamente.
    He went to the desk where he kept his documents, found them, and began
    to read them slowly.

13. Cuando ____ la puerta, se ____ con que ____ mucho más de
    lo que ____ .
    When she opened the door, she found that it was raining a lot harder than
    she expected.

14. ¿Cómo te ____ ayer? Mira, me ____ (form of **resultar**) mucho mejor
    de lo que me ____ que fuera posible.
    How did it go for you yesterday? Look, it worked out much better than
    I had imagined was possible.

15. Su padre se ____ Eliodoro Moreira. Siempre me ____ un hombre muy
    sobrio, aunque el vino no le ____ (form of **disgustar**).
    His father was named Eliodoro Moreira. He always seemed to me to be a
    very sober man, although he didn't dislike wine.

• EXERCISE B

To practice the imperfect, answer the following questions in the terms of the way
things used to be when you were ten years old.

1. ¿Dónde vivía Ud. cuando tenía diez años?
2. ¿Cómo era la casa en que vivía Ud.?
3. ¿Cuántos hermanos tenía Ud.?

4. ¿Eran mayores o menores que Ud.?
5. ¿Se llevaba Ud. bien con ellos?
6. ¿A qué escuela iba Ud.?
7. ¿Cómo era la escuela? ¿Le gustaba?
8. ¿Cuáles eran sus materias predilectas?
9. ¿Le gustaba más jugar solo(a) o con los otros niños?
10. ¿Qué juegos o deportes le gustaban más?
11. ¿Le gustaba más leer o ver la televisión?
12. ¿Cuáles eran algunos de sus libros favoritos? ¿Programas de televisión?
13. ¿Era buena cocinera su mamá (o su papá)?
14. ¿Cuál era su plato favorito?
15. ¿Le gustaba tener diez años?

• EXERCISE C

Complete the following sentences as indicated.

1. Nos _____ (form of **llevar**) bastante bien hasta que _____ lo que había
   ocurrido años antes. Después no _____ (form of **haber**) modo.
   *We were getting along pretty well until she heard what had happened years
   before. After that it was hopeless.*
2. A Carlota le _____ un tocadiscos porque ayer _____ su cumpleaños. Yo le
   _____ a mandar una tarjeta, pero no _____ encontrar una apropiada.
   *They gave Carlota a record player because yesterday was her birthday.
   I was going to send her a card, but I didn't succeed in finding a suitable one.*
3. Me _____ poco después de llegar. Los tres meses que _____ allí,
   los _____ en el hospital.
   *I got sick shortly after I arrived. The three months I was there I spent
   in the hospital.*
4. Las elecciones _____ haberse llevado a cabo con calma y orden, pero
   más tarde se _____ (form of **dar**) a conocer lo que _____ en realidad.
   *The elections seemed to have come off in a calm and orderly fashion,
   but later what actually happened became known.*
5. De repente _____ un agudo dolor en el costado izquierdo. Al abrir los
   ojos _____ que se _____ a una pequeña flechita que se _____
   (form of **asomar**) por entre los pliegues de la camisa.
   *Suddenly he felt a sharp pain in his left side. When he opened his eyes, he saw
   that it was due to a little arrow that was sticking out among the folds of his shirt.*
6. Lo _____ practicando toda la tarde y al fin se _____ (form of **dar**) por
   vencida. Nunca lo _____ a poder tocar bien.
   *She was practicing it all afternoon and finally gave up. She was never going to
   be able to play it well.*

7. Pepe _____ fantástico anoche. Los tres números que _____ me
   _____ muchísimo.
   Pepe was great last night. The three numbers he sang impressed me very much.
8. El viejo se _____ y se _____ al público presente con palabras que _____
   su disgusto.
   The old man got up and addressed the audience in words that expressed
   his displeasure.
9. Me _____ y me _____ a mi cuarto. Me _____ en el borde de la cama y
   _____ allí hasta que me _____ . _____ en todo lo que nos habíamos dicho.
   I got mad and went to my room. I sat down on the edge of the bed and was
   there till you called me. I was thinking about everything we had said to
   each other.
10. _____ estado allí parados unos quince minutos cuando se _____ cuenta
    de que no _____ solo.
    We had been standing there about fifteen minutes when he realized that he
    wasn't alone.
11. Por más que me _____ , _____ en que _____ quedarme hasta después
    de la comida.
    No matter how much I resisted, they insisted that I should stay until after
    the meal.
12. ¿Cuándo _____ que _____ a estar en Buenos Aires?
    When did you find out that you were going to be in Buenos Aires?
13. No me _____ creer que _____ las tres de la mañana cuando _____ .
    He refused to believe me that it was three in the morning when you arrived.
14. Yo _____ que _____ hacerlo si sólo lo _____ una vez más.
    I knew that you could do it if you only tried it one more time.
15. Cuando _____ los ojos, _____ que ya se _____ retirado todos.
    When I opened my eyes, I saw that all of them had left.

• EXERCISE D

Translate the following sentences.

1. I had to take off running because his dog tried to attack me.
2. No matter how much he wanted to go, he had to stay home because he
   had a cold.
3. Since he had a new car, he offered to take them to the airport.
4. If you knew that she didn't want us to go, why didn't you say so?
5. In those days we really lived well. We had everything: friends, money,
   and the time to enjoy them.
6. Please call an ambulance. There was a terrible accident at the corner.

7. I was wondering the same thing. How could he have known the result if you didn't tell him?
8. He had been bothering me until I couldn't stand it anymore, and I yelled at him.
9. I knew that you didn't know her; that's why I introduced her to you.
10. He did everything he could to evade us, but we followed his tracks until we managed to capture him.

• EXERCISE E

To practice the preterit, answer the following questions in terms of what happened on a recent school day.

1. ¿A qué hora se despertó Ud.?
2. ¿Se levantó en seguida, o volvió a dormirse?
3. ¿Se bañó Ud.? ¿Qué jabón usó?
4. ¿Se limpió los dientes? ¿Qué pasta dentífrica usó?
5. ¿Dónde tomó Ud. el desayuno?
6. ¿A qué hora salió Ud. para ir a su primera clase?
7. ¿Fue en coche, en autobús o a pie?
8. ¿Llegó a tiempo?
9. ¿A qué clases asistió Ud.?
10. ¿Cuál le gustó más? ¿Menos?
11. ¿Dónde comió Ud.?
12. ¿Qué comió? ¿Le gustó la comida?
13. ¿A qué hora volvió Ud. a casa?
14. ¿A qué hora se acostó?
15. ¿Tardó mucho en dormirse?

• EXERCISE F

Change each of the following sentences in some way so that if the verb of the main clause was in the imperfect it will now have to be in the preterit or vice versa.

Example:
Cuando Carlos era joven, **vivía** en Alemania.
De 1971 a 1978 Carlos **vivió** en Alemania.

Yo **fui** al cine anoche.
Yo **iba** al cine con frecuencia.

1. Siempre me gustaban las comidas que preparaba mi abuela.
2. Antes veía la televisión casi todos los días.
3. El año pasado viví cinco meses en el extranjero.
4. Ayer salimos para la universidad a las siete en punto.
5. La semana pasada visité a un amigo enfermo.
6. Por lo general nos hablábamos en japonés.
7. Normalmente llovía muy poco en abril y mayo.
8. Vendieron su coche y compraron uno nuevo.
9. Cuando vi a Alfonso, estaba comiendo un helado.
10. Me escribió por primera vez hace dos meses.

• EXERCISE G

Translate into Spanish:

I was about eleven years old at that time. When we got out of school, we used to meet every afternoon at the corner of the hospital, because it had a very smooth sidewalk that lent itself very well to playing figuritas. The figuritas were pieces of thick paper or cardboard, of a circular shape, that had the picture of a famous sports figure (**deportista**) pasted on them. They were boxers, soccer players, race car drivers, etc. You collected them in order to paste them in an album which, once it was full, was turned in in exchange for fantastic prizes. Besides being able to buy them in packages of five, for which you had to have money, we got them by playing for them with the other kids in the neighborhood. For that purpose we had met again that afternoon. We waited around about half an hour till Cacho arrived. We had found out the previous day that he had three figuritas which were very difficult to get, of those that hardly ever came out, and we had decided that we would play all afternoon until we got them. Cacho approached, and we realized from the look he gave us that he knew what we were after. About three hours went by until I managed to win from him two of the three that I wanted. With that he refused to continue, but it didn't matter to me, because it was already getting late, and I would have other opportunities to get the last one I needed out of him.

• EXERCISE H

Once Exercise G has been carefully checked, write a one-page composition about some incident in your past. Try to model it after Exercise G.

"Cuando yo tenía unos . . . "

The Subjunctive

Some English-speaking students of Spanish panic at the very mention of the term *subjunctive*. They seem to regard it as something totally alien and mysterious, almost impossible for an English speaker to grasp. In reality, this is far from being so, and as matter of fact, there are a few cases in which both languages use indicative and subjunctive in almost exactly the same way.

Insiste en que su marido siempre está en casa por la noche.
She insists that her husband is always at home in the evening.
(Indicative in both languages.)

Insiste en que su marido siempre esté en casa por la noche.
She insists that her husband always be at home in the evening.
(Subjunctive in both languages.)

Si es español, ha leído el *Quijote*.
If he is Spanish, he has read the Quijote.
(Indicative in both languages.)

Si fuera español, habría leído el *Quijote.*
If he were Spanish, he would have read the Quijote.
(Subjunctive in both languages.)

However, examples like these are not exactly numerous, and it is true that most of the uses of the Spanish subjunctive require some special attention.

When a verb is put in the subjunctive in Spanish, it is usually because the thing the verb expresses is regarded as being outside of reality in some way—because it hasn't happened yet, because it is something doubtful, unknown, or hypothetical, or because it is simply contrary to the way things actually are.

Se lo daré cuando llegue.
I'll give it to him when he arrives.
(But he hasn't arrived yet. His arrival has not yet become
a reality.)

Quiero que leas esta carta.
I want you to read this letter.
(And perhaps you will. But as far as this sentence is concerned,
your reading the letter is not yet a reality.)

Aunque sea inteligente, no saca buenas notas.
Even if he is intelligent, he doesn't get good grades.
(He may be intelligent, but I don't really know for sure whether he
is or not.)

Necesito un secretario que sepa sueco.
I need a secretary that knows Swedish.
(This is a hypothetical Swedish-speaking secretary. I do not have
an actual secretary in mind, nor do I even really know whether I
will be able to find such a secretary at all.)

No harías eso si Eugenio estuviera aquí.
You wouldn't do that if Eugenio were here.
(But the reality is that he's not here.)

The traditional division into subjunctive in noun clauses, subjunctive in adjective clauses, and subjunctive in adverb clauses will be used here to present the specific uses of the Spanish subjunctive, but the use of this system is not meant to suggest that there is anything essentially different about what the subjunctives in these three categories express.

The Two Past Subjunctives

Spanish originally had only one set of verb forms for the past subjunctive, the forms ending in **-se** (for example, **tomase, comiese, viniese**). In Latin and in Old Spanish, the verb forms ending in **-ra** were not subjunctive at all, but were used as a past perfect indicative: **tomara** meant **había tomado, comiera** meant **había comido, viniera** meant **había venido,** and so on. In very formal literary Spanish, these forms are occasionally used that way even today.

Later on, the **-ra** forms gradually came to be used as a sort of conditional. **Tomara** now corresponded to at least some of the uses of **tomaría; comiera** and **viniera** were more or less equivalent to **comería** and **vendría.** This usage is also still theoretically possible and, in fact, is quite common with the four verbs **deber, haber, poder,** and **querer** (**debiera** for **debería, hubiera** for **habría, pudiera** for **podría,** and **quisiera** for **querría**).

Finally the **-ra** forms came to be used as a past subjunctive, giving Modern Spanish two sets of past subjunctive verb forms: **tomara/tomase, comiera/comiese, viniera/viniese.** When used as past subjunctives (disregarding any remnants of the **-ra** forms' earlier uses as past perfects and conditionals), the two sets seem to be more or less interchangeable. In the spoken Spanish of Latin America, however, the **-ra** forms are used more widely than the **-se** forms, although both occur in formal writing.

Sequence of Tenses

In sentences in which the verb of the main clause is in the present, the future, the present perfect, or the future perfect, the subjunctive (if there is one) is normally a present subjunctive.

Le digo que se vaya.
I tell him to leave.

Le diré que se vaya.
I will tell him to leave.

Le he dicho que se vaya.
I have told him to leave.

Le habré dicho que se vaya.
I will have told him to leave.

In sentences in which the verb of the main clause is in the imperfect, the preterit, the conditional, the past perfect, or the conditional perfect, the subjunctive (if there is one) is normally a past subjunctive.

Le decía que se fuera.
I was telling him to leave.

Le dije que se fuera.
I told him to leave.

Le diría que se fuera.
I would tell him to leave.

Le había dicho que se fuera.
I had told him to leave.

Le habría dicho que se fuera.
I would have told him to leave.

Occasionally the nature of the circumstances makes it almost unavoidable to use a past subjunctive with a main verb in the present.

Siento que no vinieran.
I'm sorry (in the present) *that they didn't come* (in the past).

In cases like the above, however, many speakers tend to prefer a present perfect subjunctive.

Siento que no hayan venido.
I'm sorry they didn't come.

The Subjunctive in Noun Clauses

A clause that fills the same kind of "slot" that a noun might fill in a sentence is often referred to as a noun clause. For example, the clause "that he is sick" in the sentence "I doubt that he is sick" functions as the direct object of "I doubt" in the same way that the noun "story" does in the sentence "I doubt his story." The following are the principal situations in which the verb of a noun clause is put in the subjunctive in Spanish.

1. In sentences of the type "A wants (or doesn't want) B to do something," the thing A does or does not want B to do is put in the subjunctive. This applies to a wide variety of verbs of wanting, telling, asking, ordering, advising, permitting, forbidding, etc.

¿Quieres que te ayuden?
Do you want them to help you?

Les pidió que no me lo dijesen.
He asked them not to tell me.

Me aconsejaron que no hiciera nada.
They advised me not to do anything.

¿Por qué permites que tus hijos te hablen así?
Why do you permit your children to talk to you that way?

Le dije que no me tratara de tú.
I told her not to call me "tú."

Decir takes the indicative when it refers to passing on information rather than giving someone a command.

Nos dijo que tendríamos que esperar.
He told us we would have to wait.

But: Nos dijo que esperásemos.
He told us to wait.

Some of these verbs can also be used with an infinitive, more or less as in English. This is true especially of **dejar**, **hacer**, **mandar**, and **permitir**, and some speakers occasionally use still other verbs this way. However, it should still be noted that *most* verbs that express something that one person does or does not want another one to do (including such common verbs as **querer** and **decir**) require **que** and the subjunctive.

Hazla decir la verdad.
Make her tell the truth.

Haz que diga la verdad.
Make her tell the truth.

Nos dejó salir.
He let us leave.

Dejó que saliéramos.
He let us leave.

2. Something that is held up as the object of a subjective emotional reaction (pleasure, regret, surprise, fear) is usually put in the subjunctive.

Me alegro de que hayas podido hablar con ellos.
I'm glad you were able to talk to them.

Siento que esté enferma.
I'm sorry she's sick.

Nos extraña que no quieran ayudarnos.
We're surprised they don't want to help us.

Temían que no llegáramos a tiempo.
They were afraid we wouldn't arrive on time.

Temer is sometimes used with the indicative when there is little if any real fear or anxiety involved.

Temo que Uds. tendrán que volver más tarde.
I'm afraid you'll have to come back later.
(This is just a polite way of telling you that you'll have to come back later. I am not actually worried or fearful about it.)

With these "emotion" verbs, it is more common to use an infinitive than a clause with the subjunctive when only one subject is involved.

Siento que no hayan ido.
I'm sorry they didn't go.

But: Siento no haber ido.
I'm sorry I didn't go.

3. It is possible to overwork the concept of "doubt" as a factor in the use of the subjunctive; however, it is true that many verbs are put in the subjunctive because someone regards the thing the verbs express as in some way doubtful, untrue, or questionable.

Dudo que sean capaces de asesinar a su abuela.
I doubt that they are capable of murdering their grandmother.

Negó que lo hubiéramos visto en el baile.
He denied that we had seen him at the dance.

Note particularly examples like the following.

No creo que vendrán.
I don't think they'll come. (I'm really pretty sure they won't.)

No creo que vengan.
I don't think they'll come, (but I'm really not too sure).

¿Cree Ud. que vendrán?
Do you think they'll come? (Or do you think they won't?)

¿Cree Ud. que vengan?
Do you really think they'll come? (I am really rather inclined to doubt it.)

4. **Ojalá**, from an Arabic expression meaning "and may God be willing," is always followed by the subjunctive, never by the indicative. When **ojalá** is followed by a present subjunctive or a present perfect subjunctive, it means *I hope it's so* (in present or future time or in past time respectively). When **ojalá** is followed by a past subjunctive or a past perfect subjunctive, it means *it isn't so, but I wish it were* (in present time or in past time respectively).

¡Ojalá que sea feliz!
I hope she's happy.
(And perhaps she is, or will be.)

¡Ojalá que haya sido feliz!
I hope she was happy. (And perhaps she was.)

¡Ojalá que fuera feliz!
I wish she were happy. (But she's not.)

¡Ojalá que hubiera sido feliz!
I wish she had been happy. (But she wasn't.)

5. A considerable variety of "impersonal" expressions take the verb that follows them in the subjunctive.

Puede que llueva mañana.
It may rain tomorrow.

No es probable que lleguen hoy.
It's not likely that they'll arrive today.

Es una lástima que tu padre no esté aquí.
It's too bad your father isn't here.

Era importante que todos tomasen parte en la ceremonia.
It was important for everybody to take part in the ceremony.

Es posible que algunos no lo sepan todavía.
It's possible that some of them don't know about it yet.

"Impersonal expressions" is a handy category for practical purposes, but remember that such expressions produce subjunctives not because they are impersonal but because they contain elements of uncertainty, possibility, necessity, or emotional attitude similar to those that produce subjunctives in any other type of sentence. When such elements are absent, there is nothing to prevent an impersonal expression from being followed by the indicative.

Es verdad que sabe mucho de la astronomía.
It's true that he knows a lot about astronomy.

Es evidente que no entiende muy bien el noruego.
It's obvious he doesn't understand Norwegian very well.

Some of these impersonal expressions are occasionally used with an infinitive, much as in English. There is a slightly different shade of meaning when the infinitive rather than the subjunctive is used.

Es imposible que te ayudemos.
It is impossible for us to help you.
(For us to help you is impossible in terms of the total external picture. External circumstances make our helping you an impossibility.)

Nos es imposible ayudarte.
It is impossible for us to help you.
(Helping you is an impossibility for us personally in terms of our situation, our own needs, desires, or abilities.)

• EXERCISE A

Complete the following sentences as indicated.

1. Quiero que _____ inmediatamente.
   I want you to come immediately.
2. Me dijo que _____ aquí, pero no se lo creí. ¡Cuanto me alegro de _____ !
   He told me you were here, but I didn't believe him. How glad I am to see you!

3. Me dijeron que ＿＿ listo para comenzar.
   I was told to show up ready to begin.
4. Se supone que nos la ＿＿ si quiere que ＿＿ con ella.
   It's assumed that he will introduce her to us if he wants us to talk to her.
5. Nos rogó que no le ＿＿ nada hasta pasado mañana.
   He begged us not to tell her anything until day after tomorrow.
6. Se lo voy a decir con toda franqueza. No creo que ＿＿ la verdad.
   I'm going to tell you very frankly. I don't believe that it is the truth.
7. Espero que ＿＿ la noche mejor que yo; este calor es insoportable.
   I hope you spent the night better than I did; this heat is unbearable.
8. Sé que te lo ＿＿ por todo lo que ＿＿ sagrado, pero yo no creo
   que te ＿＿ .
   *I know he swore it to you by everything that's sacred, but I don't believe that
   he loves you.*
9. Esto sí que ＿＿ bueno, me dijo que ＿＿ aquí sin falta, y él no ＿＿ por
   ninguna parte.
   *This is really great, he told me to be here without fail, and he isn't
   anywhere around.*
10. Le recordé que me lo ＿＿ porque dudaba que se ＿＿ .
    I reminded him to bring it to me, because I doubted that he would remember.

• EXERCISE B

Combine the sentences into one compound sentence. Make the second
sentence the main clause, and the first a dependent noun clause.

> Example:
> María está aquí.
> Yo quiero eso.
> Quiero que María esté aquí.

1. Yo estaba lista. Juan me lo pidió.
2. El hermano de Margarita está enfermo. Lo siento mucho.
3. Te dicen la verdad. Eso es muy difícil.
4. Estarán aquí para la cena. Eso es probable.
5. Nosotros tenemos razón. Carlota no lo cree.
6. Estudiaron mucho para el examen. Eso era importante.
7. No estaban satisfechos con tu trabajo. Yo lo temía.
8. Trajeron todo lo que les quedaba. Eso es verdad.
9. Jorge cumplió con su palabra. Eso me agradó.

10. Se pasan la tarde mirando la televisión. No me gusta eso.
11. Alfredo no sabía lo que le preguntábamos. Eso era evidente.
12. Pepe es capáz de decirlo delante de todos. Yo lo dudo.
13. Esos dos siempre llegan tarde. Me ofende eso.
14. No me cobró más de lo debido. Yo se lo pedí.
15. No salí del país el año pasado. Ellos me lo prohibieron.

• EXERCISE C

At the beginning of each of the following sentences add something that
expresses a reaction, attitude, or opinion in regard to the statement in
question. Do not use the same introductory expression more than once, and
be sure to use both expressions that call for a subjunctive and expressions
that do not.

Example:
Pilar es muy inteligente.
Dudo que Pilar sea muy inteligente.

Hablábamos español.
A Andrés le gustaba que habláramos español.

Su tío tiene mucho dinero.
Es evidente que su tío tiene mucho dinero.

1. Cristóbal Colón descubrió América.
2. Hoy es viernes.
3. Mi tía está muy enferma.
4. Las visitas se van pronto.
5. En esa clase siempre hablan alemán.
6. Se publicó esa novela en 1963.
7. No han llegado todavía.
8. Su abuela era de Rusia.
9. Mi cuñado comía muchos champiñones *(mushrooms)*.
10. La visitas todos los días.
11. Me llamarán por teléfono en cuanto lleguen.
12. Bailaron mucho en la fiesta.
13. Paco sabía escribir a máquina.
14. Ana es la novia de Alfonso.
15. En Luisiana muchos hablan francés.

• EXERCISE D

Translate the following sentences to present orally in class.

1. I hope that he didn't hurt himself so badly that he won't be able to play.
2. I'm glad you like it because it's the last one we have left.
3. I wish they had left earlier; with this storm I don't think they'll arrive on time.
4. I don't like for you to insist on that when you know it isn't true.
5. We found out that they were arriving with two government officials.
6. They forced him to sit down and tell them everything he knew about the case.
7. It seems to me that you ought to turn it in right away if you want them to accept it from you.
8. I know that you know a lot more than you're willing to tell us.
9. Good Lord! I promised to bring it to you, and I forgot.
10. It's best for you not to tell him any more. It's too late.

• EXERCISE E

Complete the following sentences as indicated.

1. Le pedí que lo ＿＿＿ , pero se negó.
   I asked her to try it, but she refused.
2. Me es imposible ＿＿＿ aquí y allí a la vez, querida.
   It's impossible for me to be here and there at the same time, dear.
3. Es probable que ＿＿＿ tarde. Tú sabes como son ellos.
   It's probable they'll arrive late. You know how they are.
4. Negó ＿＿＿ , pero se sospecha que ＿＿＿ .
   He denied that he had gone, but it's suspected that he's lying.
5. Me alegro que se lo ＿＿＿ . Era indispensable que lo ＿＿＿ .
   I'm glad you told him. It was indispensable for him to know it.
6. Se le dijo que no se ＿＿＿ en eso, pero ella nunca hace caso.
   She was told not to meddle in that, but she never pays any attention.
7. Nos exige que ＿＿＿ todos los días.
   He demands that we participate every day.
8. Es bueno que ＿＿＿ lo que se te pide.
   It's good for you to know what is asked of you.
9. Ojalá que todo ＿＿＿ como tú crees, pero yo tengo mis dudas.
   I hope everything turns out the way you think, but I have my doubts.
10. Fue un milagro que ＿＿＿ ileso de esa situación.
    It was a miracle that you got out of that situation unharmed.

• EXERCISE F

Translate the following sentences.

1. I'm afraid it will rain if you don't take your umbrella.
2. It was a big surprise for you to say that in front of everybody.
3. The important thing is for you to draw it well.
4. I was hoping you would lend me the book.
5. I advise you not to open it till after you leave.
6. I'm glad to know it. I almost put my foot in it.
7. Make them behave if you want them to go with us.
8. It bothers him that you're so wishy-washy (form of **dejarse llevar por la corriente**).
9. They prefer that we not mention it yet.
10. He tells me not to fail to give you his most cordial regards.
11. Don't get upset (form of **afligirse**). I don't think he's arrived yet. (Two possible ways.)
12. The bad thing is that you didn't know how to say "no" to him.
13. It's true that he was here, but don't tell anybody.
14. Let's suppose he shows up. What are you going to do with him? (Two possible ways.)
15. I hope he doesn't forget to show it to you.
16. What did you want me to do? I couldn't help it.
17. It's too bad you won't accompany me.
18. It seems to me you ought to do it over (**de nuevo**).
19. It's ridiculous for you to show up in that condition.
20. Juan isn't opposed to your doing it, but he wants you to be careful.

• EXERCISE G

Answer the following questions orally, preferably in complete sentences.

1. ¿Es posible aprender una lengua extranjera sin estudiar?
2. ¿Cree Ud. que aumente más el precio de la gasolina?
3. ¿Insiste el profesor en que vengan a clase todos los días?
4. ¿Le gusta a Ud. que hablen inglés o español en la clase?
5. ¿Sabía Ud. que le iba a tocar esta pregunta?
6. ¿Cree Ud. que será fácil el ejercicio que sigue?
7. ¿No cree Ud. que mejore la situación mundial?
8. ¿Teme Ud. que su equipo pierda el próximo partido?
9. ¿Le gustaría que alguien le regalara un auto nuevo?

10. ¿Les exige su profesor que tengan las respuestas preparadas de antemano?
11. ¿Es posible que haya vida en el planeta Marte?
12. Después de haber estudiado el subjuntivo, ¿qué aspecto de la gramática española prefiere Ud. que estudiemos?
13. ¿Es necesario que un pianista practique todos los días?
14. ¿Le gustaría que todos sus amigos estudiaran algún idioma extranjero?
15. ¿Quién quiere Ud. que sea el próximo presidente de los Estados Unidos?
16. ¿Es probable que haya un terremoto en nuestra ciudad mañana?
17. Cuando Ud. era niño, ¿dudaba que existiera el Papá Noel?
18. ¿Alguien le recomendó que estudiara español en vez de otro idioma? ¿Quién?
19. Si Ud. fuera uno de los consejeros del presidente de este país, ¿qué le aconsejaría que hiciese?
20. ¿Le parece justo que no saquen buenas notas todos los estudiantes?

• EXERCISE H

Read the following letter carefully, identifying all noun clauses and justifying the use of subjunctive or indicative in each case.

Buenos Aires, 22 de noviembre de 1977

Sr. Ricardo González
Gerente General
Autobuses del Pacífico
Cartagena, Colombia

Estimado Sr. González:

Nos dirigimos a Ud. para rogarle que trate de resolver el contratiempo ocasionado a nuestros clientes al contratar el servicio de autobuses que Ud. representa.

Aunque ha transcurrido ya algún tiempo desde que ocurrió el incidente al cual nos referimos, no hemos podido hasta ahora encontrarle una solución satisfactoria. Creemos por lo tanto que es hora de que sepa Ud. lo que en realidad sucedió ese día. No es que queramos imponerle nuestro punto de vista, pero tenemos la certeza de que una vez que oiga Ud. nuestra versión, podrá llegar a una conclusión justa y apropiada. Según nosotros hemos podido averiguar, no existe la menor duda de que la responsabilidad por los gastos extras incurridos por nuestros clientes yace con el chofer del autobús. Para llegar a esta conclusión, hemos hablado con cada uno de los pasajeros del autobús y les hemos pedido además que presenten por escrito su versión de los acontecimientos del día en cuestión. También le pedimos al chofer que presentara su versión, y es probable que él pueda ofrecer ciertos datos pertinentes al caso, pero hasta el momento él se ha negado. Esperamos que comprenda Ud., por lo tanto, por qué nos es necesaria su intervención.

Los requisitos establecidos al contratar al chofer fueron tres. Primero, que fuera puntual. Segundo, que conociera la ruta indicada para el viaje. Tercero, que estuviera en el lugar indicado para el viaje de regreso. Según las indicaciones que tenemos, dicho chofer no cumplió con ninguno de los tres, ya que llegó con una hora de retraso para la salida, se perdió varias veces en ruta, y lo más lamentable, no apareció por ninguna parte para el viaje de regreso. Esto último ocasionó que el grupo de pasajeros tuviera que encontrarse otros medios de transporte para completar su viaje. Confiamos en que, basado en esta información, llegará Ud. a la misma conclusión que nosotros, y le rogamos, por lo tanto, nos haga llegar un cheque en la cantidad de $237.00 para cubrir los gastos extras incurridos por nuestros clientes.

Agradecidos por su atención, quedamos en espera de su respuesta.

Sinceramente,

Luis Molina

Luis Molina
Gerente de viajes

Now, 1) compose a letter from Mr. González replying to Mr. Molina's letter, or 2) imagine a different incident and write a letter of complaint or protest resulting from it. In either case, make an effort to use as many noun clauses as possible.

Subjunctive in Adjective Clauses

In the sentence "The man who is eating a rutabaga is my brother," the expression "who is eating a rutabaga" describes the man in very much the same way that the adjective "bald" describes the man in the sentence "The bald man is my brother." "Who is eating a rutabaga" can therefore be referred to as an adjective clause.

In Spanish, if a sentence implies that it is not known to what, if anything, the description contained in an adjective clause applies, then the verb of the adjective clause is put in the subjunctive.

Necesito un libro que explique bien la gramática generativa.
I need a book that explains generative grammar well.
(I do not have a particular book in mind. In fact, I do not really know whether such a book is even available.)

¿Conoces a alguien que haya estado en Moscú?
Do you know anybody who has been in Moscow?
(If I am having to ask, I evidently do not know whether you know such a person, much less who it is.)

The verb of an adjective clause is also put in the subjunctive if the implication is that there isn't anything (at least in the context of the sentence) to which the description applies.

No conocen a nadie que hable flamenco.
They don't know anybody that speaks Flemish.
(There undoubtedly exist people who speak Flemish, but they do not know any such person.)

Aquí no hay nada que me guste.
There isn't anything here that I like.

The "who" of "the man who is eating a rutabaga" is known in traditional grammatical terminology as a relative pronoun, and "man" is said to be its antecedent. In those terms, the rules just given can be stated as follows: if the antecedent of a relative pronoun is *indefinite* (unknown or hypothetical) or *negative* (nonexistent), then the verb of the clause that the relative pronoun introduces is put in the subjunctive.

A similar principle of "indefiniteness" governs the use of indicative or subjunctive in sentences like the following, even though the sentences do not actually contain adjective clauses.

Iremos adonde tú quieres.
We'll go where you want us to.
(And it is known where that is.)

Iremos adonde tú quieras.
We'll go wherever you want us to.
(Wherever that may turn out to be.)

Note, for instance, the similarity of the above examples to the following ones which do contain adjective clauses.

Te daré el libro que quieres.
I'll give you the book you want.
(It is known which book that is.)

Te daré el libro que quieras.
I'll give you whichever book you want.

• EXERCISE A

Complete the following sentences as indicated.

1. Busquemos uno que _____ (tener) letra más grande porque no alcanzo a leerlo.

2. ¿Dónde está el señor que _____ (tener) las llaves del cuarto?
3. No hay nadie que _____ (cantar) como tú, mi amor.
4. Hay alguien aquí que lo _____ (saber), y quiero que me lo _____ (decir).
5. A pesar de lo que le _____ (decir), ella nunca hace caso.
6. Necesito encontrar una persona que me _____ (entender); si no, me vuelvo loco.
7. Tráigame al señor que _____ (hablar) urdu; yo no entiendo nada de eso.
8. ¿Hay una tienda que _____ (vender) yerba mate? Sí, hay una que _____ (quedar) en la calle Rivadavia.
9. Me gustan las dos, pero invitaré a la que _____ (contestar) primero.
10. Estudia cuanto te _____ (ser) necesario para aprobar.

• EXERCISE B

Change each of the following sentences so that if the verb of the relative clause is in the indicative it will now have to be put in the subjunctive or vice versa.

Example:
No hay nada aquí que me guste.
Hay muchas cosas aquí que me gustan.

1. Tengo un amigo que es malabarista *(juggler)*.
2. Hay muchos restaurantes en esta ciudad donde sirven comida vietnamita.
3. Necesitamos un libro que explique la diferencia entre **ser** y **estar**.
4. Mi tío busca un cocinero que sepa preparar el mole poblano.
5. Joaquín no encontró ningún coche que no fuera demasiado caro.
6. Anoche vi un programa de televisión que me gustó mucho.
7. No conozco a nadie que haya visto un platillo volante.
8. Mi abuelo era un hombre que hablaba muchos idiomas.
9. ¿Hay alguien aquí que conozca a Matilde Sánchez?
10. En la sala de espera había una señorita que leía una revista.

• EXERCISE C

Translate the following sentences to present orally in class.

1. We want a receptionist that knows how to speak Spanish.
2. Introduce me to the man who has lived in that region; I need to ask him something.

3. I would like to accommodate you (form of **complacer**), but nobody exists who has all that information (**datos**).
4. Anything he does turns out well for him.
5. Why are you asking *me?* Isn't there anybody else that can help you with that?
6. He ordered the food that he liked best, but it was all gone.
7. There's no actor that does that role better.
8. Years ago there was a gentleman that knew how to fix (form of **componer**) those gadgets (**aparatos**), but not any more.
9. In Mexico City I know a restaurant where they serve Argentine food.
10. We will let only those who know how to dance very well participate.

• EXERCISE D

Complete the following sentences as indicated.

1. Los que _____ terminado pueden irse. No se olviden de traer lo que _____ para mañana.
   Those who have finished can leave. Don't forget to bring what I asked you for tomorrow.
2. Encontremos un cuarto que _____ desocupado para tener la reunión.
   Let's find a room that's unoccupied in order to hold the meeting.
3. El que más me _____ es el rubio que _____ sentado al lado de la fuente.
   The one I like the best is the blond that is sitting beside the fountain.
4. Perdóname el dolor que mis palabras te _____ causado.
   Forgive me the pain my words may have caused you.
5. ¿Cuál es el autobús que _____ al zócalo?
   Which is the bus that goes to the zócalo (public square)?
6. Cómprate un auto que _____ más rápido; con éste no llegamos nunca.
   Buy yourself a car that goes faster; with this one we'll never get there.
7. Pide lo que _____. Hoy pago yo porque me saqué el grande de la lotería.
   Order whatever you want to. I'm paying today because I won the grand prize in the lottery.
8. No había ni un libro que _____ la pena leer dos veces.
   There wasn't even one book that was worth reading twice.
9. La que lo _____ mejor recibirá el premio prometido.
   Whichever one paints it best will receive the prize announced.
10. El día que le _____ eso, se acaba todo.
    The day you tell him that, it's all over.

• EXERCISE E

Translate the following sentences.

1. There's nobody that can help me get out of this mess (**lío**).
2. If I'm not mistaken, there's someone in Buenos Aires who still remembers having seen him.
3. No matter what you say, I don't like that lady.
4. Will you lend me a pen? I'm sorry, I don't have one that writes.
5. No matter what they ask for, don't give them anything until you receive the captain's order.
6. Let's try to find someone who has been to Colombia and we'll ask him.
7. In spite of what you say, it's necessary to do it carefully.
8. Nowadays it's difficult to find a politician who is in the habit of (form of **acostumbrar**) telling the truth.
9. In that game the ones that shout loudest win.
10. Bring me the one that's on the table. I want to finish it before starting on the other one.
11. There's always going to be somebody who knows more than you do.
12. Let's see if we find a restaurant where you can get a good paella.
13. Take all the ones you want. We've already finished with them.
14. There has to be somebody that knows how that is prepared.
15. No matter now much you may insist, I can't consent to it.

• EXERCISE F

Answer the following questions in complete sentences.

1. ¿Tiene Ud. algún amigo que hable chino?
2. ¿Conoce Ud. a alguien que haya estado en la Antártida?
3. ¿Ha visto últimamente alguna película que no le haya gustado para nada?
4. ¿Le gustaría tener un amigo que supiera tocar la guitarra?
5. ¿Hay aspectos de la gramática española que Ud. encuentre difíciles?
6. ¿Sabe Ud. si hay países en que coman perros?
7. Cuando Ud. era niño, ¿tenía compañeros que no fueran norteamericanos?
8. ¿Hay razas de perros que no tengan cola (tail)?
9. ¿Hay estados en este país donde cultiven arroz?
10. ¿Había una escuela en la ciudad donde Ud. nació en la que enseñaran ruso?

• EXERCISE G

Read the following paragraphs carefully. Identify all adjective clauses and justify the use of subjunctive or indicative in those clauses.

¿Dices que quieres que te diga algo sobre las cosas que yo quisiera tener y que no tengo? Pues, vamos a ver. Bueno, para empezar, me gustaría tener más amigos que hablaran español. Es difícil aprender una lengua cuando no hay nadie con quien practicar. Cuando yo estudiaba francés, parecía que tenía muchos amigos que hablaban español, y ninguno que hablara francés. Ahora que estudio español, me encuentro con un sin número de personas que hablan francés, y los que hablaban español han desaparecido como por arte de magia.

¿Qué más hay que yo necesite? Pues no estaría mal tener un coche que diera por lo menos 30 millas por galón de gasolina. Ninguno de los que yo he tenido hasta ahora ha podido dar más de 12 millas por galón. Y sería muy bueno también tener uno que funcionara más de 50 millas sin descomponerse. ¿Algo más? Bueno, casi no quiero ni decirlo, pero si fuera posible, me gustaría mucho tener un libro de español que tuviera ejercicios menos ridículos que los que tiene el que estamos usando ahora. ¡Imagínate pedirle a uno que escriba una composición sobre las cosas que necesita pero no tiene!

Now write a similar paragraph or two (perhaps about things you don't have but would like to have) in which you use as many adjective clauses as reasonably possible.

6

Subjunctive in Adverb Clauses

1. In clauses introduced by time expressions such as **cuando** *(when)*, **hasta que** *(until)*, **en cuanto**, **luego que**, **tan pronto como**, and **así que** *(as soon as)*, and **después (de) que** *(after)*, the verb is put in the subjunctive if what it expresses had not yet happened at the time in question.

Esperamos hasta que llegaron.
We waited until they arrived.
(We waited, and they arrived.)

But: Prometimos esperar hasta que llegasen.
We promised to wait until they arrived.
(At the time we made the promise, they hadn't arrived yet.)

En cuanto llegó, le di los arándanos.
As soon as he arrived, I gave him the cranberries.
(He arrived, and I gave him the cranberries.)

But: En cuanto llegue, le daré los arándanos.
As soon as he arrives, I will give him the cranberries.
(But he hasn't arrived yet.)

Note that **antes (de) que** *(before)* is *always* followed by the subjunctive and does not come under this rule.

Les mostré el tapiz antes de que se fueran.
I showed them the tapestry before they left.

When **mientras** means *while,* it usually does not take the subjunctive, even when it refers to something still in the future. It does take the subjunctive when it means *as long as* and refers to something extending into the future.

Tocaremos discos mientras los invitados comen.
We will play records while the guests are eating.

Mientras tengan dinero, se divertirán.
As long as they have money, they'll enjoy themselves.

Verbs expressing things that happen regularly are usually put in the indicative. (Since the implication is that these things have happened in the past and will continue to happen *in the future,* English-speaking students are sometimes tempted to put them in the subjunctive.)

Siempre voy al Museo del Prado cuando estoy en Madrid.
I always go to the Prado Museum when I'm in Madrid.

2. In practice, **aunque** *(although, even though, even if)* is probably followed by the subjunctive more than by the indicative. In theory, however, **aunque** takes the indicative if whatever it introduces is presented as being a definitely established fact.

Aunque no le guste a tu tío, la fiesta va a ser en el apartamento de él.
*Even if your uncle doesn't like it, the party is going to be at
his apartment.*
(It is not definitely known whether he will like it or not.)

Aunque duran poco, me gustan mucho las rosas.
Even though they don't last long, I like roses a great deal.
(I regard it as a known and accepted fact that roses don't last long.)

For some speakers of English, the use of *even if* in English seems to correspond fairly well to the use of **aunque** + subjunctive in Spanish, while *even though* corresponds to **aunque** + indicative. Consider the following examples.

Aunque sea caro, voy a comprarlo.
*Even if it is expensive (and I don't know for sure whether it is or not),
I'm going to buy it.*

Aunque es caro, voy a comprarlo.
*Even though it is expensive (and I know that it actually is), I'm
going to buy it.*

3. Several expressions are best remembered as simply always being followed
by the subjunctive.

Robamos el brillante **sin que** ella lo supiera.
We stole the diamond without her knowing about it.

Te lo diré a ti **con tal (de) que** no se lo digas a Pancracio.
I'll tell you provided you don't tell Pancracio.

Iremos a la pinacoteca **a menos que** granice.
We'll go to the picture gallery unless it hails.

Le di la carta **para que (a fin de que)** la leyera.
I gave her the letter so she could read it (in order for her to read it).

Como si *(as if)* is always followed by the subjunctive, but only by the
past or past perfect subjunctive.

Camina como si estuviera enfermo.
He walks as if he were sick. (Or: He walks as if he is sick.)

Habló de la novela como si la hubiera leído.
She talked about the novel as if she had read it.

4. In many parts of the Spanish-speaking world, **como** can be used with
the subjunctive to mean *provided, so long as.*

Como no es muy tarde, iré a verlos.
Since it isn't very late, I'll go see them.

But: Como no sea tarde, iré a verlos.
Provided (If) it isn't too late, I'll go see them.

• EXERCISE A

Complete the following sentences as indicated.

1. Como _____ (trabajar) hasta tarde anoche, se siente muy mal esta mañana.

2. Te lo presto con tal que me lo _____ (devolver) cuando yo lo _____ (necesitar).
3. Antes de que me _____ (olvidar), quiero mostrarte lo que me trajeron del Japón.
4. Ya que tú _____ (tener) dos, nos puedes facilitar el que no vas a usar.
5. Ahora que yo _____ (comprender) esa cuestión, se la voy a explicar a todos con mucho ciudado para que nos _____ (apoyar) en las elecciones.
6. Aunque _____ (querer) ayudarte, no se lo permitirá su respeto a las convenciones sociales.
7. Antes de _____ (esparcir) esos rumores, trata de establecer su veracidad.
8. La verdad es que se lo pasamos a Pepe sin que ella nos _____ (ver).
9. No hace falta que vuelvas por aquí hasta que _____ (estar) dispuesto a cooperar con la junta directiva.
10. Por mal que _____ (cantar), muchacha, nos conmueven tus canciones.

ᐧ EXERCISE B

Modify the following sentences by changing the verb of the main clause to the tense indicated and making all other necessary changes.

1. Hablé con Ricardo cuando estuvo en California. (future)
2. Seguirá practicando hasta que le salga bien. (past)
3. En cuanto comimos, nos trajeron la cuenta. (future)
4. Cuando tengamos todo preparado, te avisaremos. (past)
5. Tan pronto como me lo dijeron, se lo hice saber a Carlota. (future)
6. Luego que termines de estudiar, podemos ir al partido. (past)
7. Se va a bajar de ahí antes de que se caiga. (past)
8. Siempre que estudiaba, salía muy bien en el examen. (present)
9. Te prestará su abrigo para que te protejas del frío. (past)
10. Consiguieron pasar el río sin que los observara la patrulla. (future)
11. Le dijimos que iríamos a verlos a menos que estuviéramos muy cansados. (future)
12. Van a venir con tal que los invitemos. (past)
13. Jorge promete pasar a buscarte a no ser que llueva. (past)
14. Lo iba a ver aunque me fuera muy penoso. (future)
15. Lo fui a ver aunque me era muy penoso. (future)

• EXERCISE C

Translate the following sentences to present orally in class.

1. They couldn't finish it because they had to wait until you arrived.

2. Please let me know (form of **avisarme**) as soon as you know the result.
3. They all stood up so she wouldn't feel so uncomfortable.
4. Those flowers won't stop blooming as long as there's sun to protect them from the cold.
5. When the official arrives, act dumb (form of **hacerse el distraído**) and don't pay any attention to whatever he may ask you.
6. Even though she knows a lot, I can't stand (form of **aguantar**) that teacher.
7. So as not to offend him, nobody dares to tell him the truth.
8. As soon as he opened his mouth, we knew that he was going to say something outrageous (**algún disparate**).
9. You can consider that all has been lost unless someone comes to our rescue.
10. One must proceed as (**según**) the rules of the game indicate.

• EXERCISE D

Complete the following sentences as indicated.

1. Se lo dije de una vez para que no me _____ (molestar) nunca más con esas preguntas impertinentes.
2. Llegó antes de lo que yo _____ (esperar) y se llevó todo lo que les quedaba.
3. Es increíble que una persona de su talla _____ (decir) eso, a menos que se lo _____ (obligar) las terribles circunstancias en que se encuentra.
4. Como _____ (confiar) en ella, le es muy fácil hacerles creer cualquier cosa.
5. Hazlo de tal manera (in such a way) que ni el más fastidioso _____ (poder) encontrarle falla.
6. Cuando te _____ (sentir) mejor, dame una llamada y nos reuniremos para finalizar el trato.
7. No te aflijas, tú hazlo como _____ (creer) que debe ser, y luego veremos lo que resulta.
8. No podemos permitir que siga por ese camino sin que alguien le _____ (advertir) de los peligros que yacen en él.
9. Está bien que ella lo acompañe con tal que Ud. _____ (ser) responsable por su salud.
10. Alcanzó a decirlo, pero no sin que lo _____ (traicionar) la voz.

• EXERCISE E

Translate the following sentences.

1. I love you even if you're ugly.
2. You have to present it to them in such a way that they'll accept it right away, otherwise we're through (form of **estar listos**).
3. Unless she was lying, which didn't seem likely to me, things were going to come out really, really well (**requetebién**).
4. I want you to be at my side because my sight is already failing me (form of **faltarme**).
5. As soon as he found out what had happened to you, he became furious and went out to look for those who were responsible.
6. Since the young lady in blue knows so much, maybe she wants to come up front (**pasar al frente**) to explain it to us.
7. Before that happens, you have to try once more to find a peaceful solution.
8. It's essential (**indispensable**) for them to receive the documents tonight so that tomorrow they'll give us their answer.
9. I arrived as soon as possible, but not before she had left.
10. When you're my age, you'll understand that all that glitters is not gold.

• EXERCISE F

Answer the following questions using a dependent adverbial clause in your reply.

1. ¿Hasta cuándo piensa Ud. seguir estudiando español?
2. ¿Prefiere Ud. que el profesor les explique la lección antes de que la lean los alumnos o después?
3. ¿Van a terminar de hacer este ejercicio antes de que suene el timbre?
4. ¿Qué piensa hacer en cuanto termine esta clase?
5. ¿Se preparan Uds. para la clase todos los días sin que se lo exija el profesor?
6. ¿Qué planes tiene para después de que Ud. se reciba?
7. ¿En qué pensaba Ud. mientras su compañero contestaba la pregunta anterior?
8. ¿Para qué les exige su profesor que contesten estas preguntas?
9. ¿Qué daría Ud. para poder hablar español como si fuera su propia lengua?
10. Cuando Ud. era niño, ¿se imaginó alguna vez que se encontraría en estas circunstancias?
11. ¿Qué sería Ud. capaz de hacer para que su familia no pasara hambre?
12. ¿Es fácil hacer trampas en un juego sin que nadie se dé cuenta?

13. ¿Se negaría Ud. a traducir una carta del español al inglés a menos que se lo pagasen?
14. ¿Está Ud. dispuesto a seguir estudiando español con tal que no saque malas notas?

• EXERCISE G

Read the following paragraph carefully. Identify all adverbial clauses and justify the use of the subjunctive or indicative in each case.

¡Pobre Lázaro! Quiere muchísimo a su familia y dice que no podrá ser realmente feliz mientras que ellos no lo sean. Pero temo que para cuando eso se convierta en realidad, él estará ya muerto o sin un centavo, o las dos cosas. Consuelo, por ejemplo, la hija mayor, anunció que no estaría satisfecha hasta que aprendiera a hablar francés. Por lo tanto, Lázaro gastó un dineral para que ella estudiara francés en las mejores universidades americanas, y una fortuna para que pudiera ir a Francia a perfeccionarse. Una vez allí, aunque sí aprendió a hablar francés perfectamente, también se enamoró de un desconocido poeta existencialista. Hace cinco años que no se sabe nada de ella.

José Luis, el único hijo de Lázaro, decidió que aunque la carrera universitaria le costara otra fortuna a su padre, no podría ser feliz a menos que consiguiera ser la autoridad máxima en cuestion de avispas *(wasps)*. Y todo iba bastante bien hasta que el médico determinó que José Luis tenía una incurable alergia a toda especie de himenópteros *(hymenoptera)*.

Claro que también existe el caso de las tres hijas menores, sin ni siquiera mencionar el de su señora. En caso de que a Ud. le interesen los problemas que Lázaro ha tenido con ellas, no tiene más que preguntárselo y él se lo contará con todo gusto. Solamente le pido que por favor no se lo pregunte cuando yo esté presente. Es que me da no sé qué ver llorar a un hombre ya grande.

Now, 1) write a similar paragraph in which you describe how Lázaro's wife has reacted to this deplorable situation, or 2) describe the problems poor Lázaro has had with each of the three younger daughters.

Subjunctive in Conditional Sentences

Note the use of tenses in the following types of conditional sentences.

1. In a simple, neutral conditional sentence there is no particular implication that whatever the "if-clause" expresses is necessarily either likely or unlikely. Such sentences do not take the subjun̈̈e at all.

Si estaban en el baile, no los vi.
If they were at the dance, I didn't see them.
(Maybe they were, maybe they weren't.)

Mañana iremos al parque si no llueve.
Tomorrow we'll go to the park if it doesn't rain.
(Maybe it will, maybe it won't.)

2. In a "contrary-to-fact" conditional sentence the implication is that whatever the if-clause expresses is definitely not so. In such sentences Spanish uses the past subjunctive in the if-clause and the conditional in the main clause.

Si supiera inglés, leería *La cabaña del tío Tom.*
If she knew English (but she doesn't), she would read Uncle Tom's Cabin.

Les habría dado el dinero si me lo hubieran pedido.
*I would have given them the money if they had asked me for it
(but they didn't).*

3. English distinguishes a third type of conditional sentence (sometimes designated in traditional Latin textbooks by the quaint but informative name of "future less vivid") in which whatever the if-clause expresses is presented as possible but not especially likely. Spanish treats such sentences exactly the same as contrary-to-fact sentences: past subjunctive in the if-clause and conditional in the main clause.

Si encontramos el libro, tendremos que devolvérselo.
*If we find the book (maybe we will, maybe we won't), we'll have
to give it back to him.*
(No subjunctive.)

But: Si encontrásemos el libro, tendríamos que devolvérselo.
*If we should find (if we were to find) the book, we would have to
give it back to him.*
(Apparently our finding the book is not regarded as particularly
probable. But it could happen, and if it should, this would be the result.)

In the sentence "If he goes to Granada, he will visit the Alhambra," English-speakers are often tempted to put "if he goes to Granada" in the subjunctive in Spanish. They reason that his trip to Granada is still in the future, is not yet a reality, and in fact may never take place at all, all of which ought to add up to a subjunctive. Perhaps these reasons ought to add up to a subjunctive, but unfortunately in Spanish usage they don't. *Never use present subjunctive in the if-clause of a conditional sentence.* If the sentence is not of a type that calls for the *past* subjunctive in the if-clause, don't use subjunctive at all.

All of the foregoing applies only to actual conditional sentences: if X is so, then Y will be so; if A were true, then B would be true, etc. It does not apply to another type of sentence in which *if* (**si**) really means 'whether': No sé si viene = *I don't know if he's coming* = *I don't know whether he's coming.* In fact, some speakers even use present subjunctive after **si** in "whether" sentences: No sé si venga.

• EXERCISE A

Some of the following conditional sentences present a neutral condition: "If it rains we won't go"; "If I have the money, I'll take a trip to Europe." Others present an unlikely condition—"If it were to rain, we wouldn't go"—or a contrary-to-fact condition—"If I had the money (but I don't), I would take a trip to Europe." Change each sentence to express the opposite of what it now does.

Example:
Si llueve no iremos.
Si lloviera no iríamos.

Si tuviera el dinero iría a Europa.
Si tengo el dinero iré a Europa.

1. Si hablan inglés, podré charlar con ellos.
2. Si Felipe llega antes de las cinco, podrá acompañarnos.
3. No estudiaré medicina si se oponen mis padres.
4. No nos lo diría Teresa si no fuera la verdad.
5. Si no les pareciese justo, no lo pagarían.
6. Si se murió el año pasado, nadie me lo dijo.
7. Si no tenían dinero, comían en casa.
8. ¿Cuándo llegarán si vienen en tren?
9. No nos acompañarán si están enfermos.
10. Les prestaríamos el dinero si lo tuviéramos.

• EXERCISE B

Combine each pair of sentences which follows into: 1) a neutral conditional sentence (present or future); 2) an unlikely or contrary-to-fact conditional sentence (present or future); and 3) a contrary-to-fact conditional sentence (past).

Example:
Tengo que estudiar. No podemos ir al cine.

1) Si tengo que estudiar, no podremos ir al cine. (future)
2) Si tuviera que estudiar, no podríamos ir al cine. (future)
3) Si hubiera tenido que estudiar, no hubiéramos podido ir al cine. (past)

1. Hoy tengo examen. Voy a salir mal.
2. La fiesta está muy animada. Los vecinos se quejan.
3. Tenemos un auto nuevo. Te llevamos al aeropuerto.
4. Marta sale con Jorge. Yo estoy muy disgustado.
5. La carne está muy cocida. No la puedo comer.
6. Me duele mucho la cabeza. Me voy a acostar.

7. Paco pone los discos colombianos. Todos bailamos mucho.
8. El profesor está enojado. Los alumnos se callan.
9. Esta lección es fácil. Yo la aprendo en seguida.
10. La silla está desocupada. Tú puedes sentarte en ella.

• EXERCISE C

Complete the following sentences as indicated.

1. Si _____ ayudarme con esto, ponte esos guantes para no ensuciarte.
   If you want to help me with this, put on those gloves so you won't get dirty.
2. Si _____ traérmelo en seguida, te lo agradecería inmensamente.
   If you could bring it to me right away, I would be extremely grateful to you.
3. Si no me _____ metido en esto, no _____ sabido lo que es sufrir.
   If I hadn't gotten into this, I wouldn't have known what it is to suffer.
4. Si no _____ cooperar con nosotros, puede retirarse.
   If he doesn't want to cooperate with us, he can withdraw.
5. Si _____ sospechado que Ud. se iba a aprovechar de ellos de ese modo,
   no les _____ permitido presentarse solos.
   *If I had suspected that you were going to take advantage of them in that
   way, I wouldn't have permitted them to show up alone.*
6. Si María _____ eso, es porque _____ que _____ así.
   If Maria said that, it's because she knows it's that way.
7. Si yo _____ eso, lo _____ que pagar caramente.
   If I did that, I would have to pay for it dearly.
8. No le _____ podido ocurrir esto si Ud. _____ estado aquí como prometió.
   This couldn't have happened to you if you had been here as you promised.
9. Si _____ traído más dinero, ahora no nos _____ en esta situación.
   *If we had brought more money, now we wouldn't find ourselves in
   this situation.*
10. _____ mañana mismo si Ud. _____ dispuesto a hablar con ella.
    We will go tomorrow for sure if you are willing to talk to her.

• EXERCISE D

Translate the following sentences.

1. He's studying as if he were going to have an exam in the (**un**) not too
   distant future.
2. What would Josefina do if I told her that the last boat for Calamuchita
   has already left?

3. If you prepared that lesson, you won't have any trouble (**problema**) explaining it to us.
4. If there had been more time, I could have brought you the one you asked us for.
5. I don't know if he wants to come or not; he refuses to tell us his preference.
6. If he should (if he were to) call again (form of **volver a** + infinitive), please get in touch with me (form of **comunicarse con**) no matter where I may be.
7. If you're not better tomorrow, stay in bed.
8. Why were you afraid to see her (**verse con ella**) if it wasn't true that you had deceived her?
9. That lady talks as if they had wound her up (form of **dar cuerda**).
10. I can't find my checkbook (**libreta de cheques**); if it should show up (form of **llegar a aparecer**) around there, please keep it for me until I return.

• EXERCISE E

Answer the following questions in Spanish.

1. ¿Dónde come Ud. si tiene poco dinero?
2. ¿Cuál habría sido su profesión si hubiese vivido en el siglo dieciséis?
3. Si Ud. fuera de Austria, ¿cuál sería su lengua materna?
4. ¿Cometería Ud. un crimen si se lo pidiera su mejor amigo?
5. Si le concedieran una beca *(scholarship)* para estudiar en Groenlandia, ¿la aceptaría Ud.?
6. ¿Cuál habría sido su nacionalidad si hubiese nacido en Leningrado?
7. ¿Cuál es la obra literaria más importante que Ud. no podría leer en el original si no supiera español?
8. Si nevara mañana, ¿se quedaría Ud. en casa?
9. Si Ud. se aburre en una clase, ¿se lo dice al profesor?
10. ¿En qué país le gustaría haber nacido si no hubiera nacido en los Estados Unidos?

• EXERCISE F

Read the following passage carefully and observe all the different verb uses.

Mañana llega la tía Amalia para su visita anual. ¡Cómo la odio a ella! ¡Cómo odio sus visitas! Claro que la culpa es mía, porque si no la hubiera invitado, no vendría. Pero yo soy su sobrino favorito (si es que puedo creerle las cosas que me dice), y si no la invito todos los años, se enoja y me dice que va a cambiar su testamento. Y si cambia el testamento, yo no heredo su dinero. Y si es cierto que tiene tanto dinero como dicen, definitivamente quiero heredarlo. ¡Sería terrible que yo tuviera que quedarme tan pobre para el resto de la vida! Si viviera en una casa realmente grande, la podría hacer quedar en el "suite" rosado, o en el ala este de la casa, o en cualquier otro lugar donde tal vez no tuviera que estar con ella todo el tiempo. Pero si uno vive en un apartamento pequeño como el mío, no hay cómo quitarse de encima a una visita no muy apreciada. Creo que le voy a escribir y decir que he caído enfermo de alguna enfermedad exótica como la lepra o la plaga bubónica. Pero si le digo eso, ¿me creerá? ¡Seguro que no! Era igual cuando yo era niño; si trataba de decirle cualquier mentirita, ella siempre se daba cuenta. Tal vez si le dijera que me he vuelto vegetariano y le sirviera nada más que soyas y verduras crudas no se quedaría mucho tiempo. Y supongo que si nada da resultado, puedo hacer lo que hice durante su última visita, aunque de veras es un modo tan terrible de tratar a una persona, aún a la tía Amalia.

Now, 1) write a passage of equal length which describes Aunt Amalia's visit, or 2) modeled after the above passage, write a one-page composition in which you use correctly as many if-clauses as possible.

Commands

Direct Commands

Command is the term ordinarily used in Spanish textbooks to refer to any verb form used by one person to tell another person directly to do something: **dime la verdad, siéntense, levante la mano**, etc. The question of commands is a little more complicated in Spanish than in English since in Spanish the verb form varies depending on whether the command is singular or plural, polite or familiar, and (in the case of familiar commands) affirmative or negative.

Most commands in Spanish are expressed by means of the appropriate form of the present subjunctive. For example, the present subjunctive is used for *all* "polite" or "formal" commands (**usted** and **ustedes**), whether they are affirmative ("do!") or negative ("don't!").

Tráigame el dinero mañana.
Bring me the money tomorrow.
(Polite and affirmative.)

No lean esa carta.
Don't read that letter.
(Polite and negative.)

Furthermore, the present subjunctive is used for *all* negative ("don't") commands, whether they are polite or familiar.

No se enoje.
Don't get mad.
(Polite and negative.)

No digas eso.
Don't say that.
(Familiar and negative.)

The only Spanish commands that are *not* expressed by present subjunctive forms are commands that are both familiar (**tú** and **vosotros**) and affirmative ("do!" rather than "don't!"). These use special forms that are generally referred to as the *imperative*. Perhaps the easiest way to remember the forms of the **tú** imperative is to note that for all verbs except a small number of irregular ones (decir/**di**, hacer/**haz**, ir/**ve**, poner/**pon**, salir/**sal**, ser/**sé**, tener/**ten**, valer/**val**, venir/**ven**), these commands are identical to the forms of the third person singular ("he-she-it") of the present indicative: **habla, come, escribe, duerme**. (This similarity is simply a coincidence; there is no actual connection, historical or otherwise, between the two forms.) The **vosotros** imperative of *all* Spanish verbs is like the infinitive except that it ends in **-d** rather than **-r**: **hablad, comed, escribid**. Except in **idos** *go away* (from **irse**), the **d** of this form drops when the reflexive pronoun **os** follows it: **sentaos, comprendeos, dormíos**. (In colloquial peninsular Spanish the **vosotros** imperative is often replaced by the infinitive: **sentaros, comer, escribir** for **sentaos, comed, escribid**.)

The use of various verb forms to express commands in Spanish may be summarized as follows:

1. Commands in the present subjunctive (all Ud. and Uds. commands and all negative commands):

¡Hable (Ud.)!   ¡No hable (Ud.)!
¡Hablen (Uds.)!   ¡No hablen (Uds.)!
¡No hables (tú)!
¡No habléis (vosotros)!

2. Commands in the imperative (**tú** and **vosotros** affirmative commands):

¡Habla (tú)!
¡Hablad (vosotros)!

Object pronouns follow affirmative commands (either subjunctive or imperative) and precede negative commands: **despiértese**, **no se despierte**; **despiértate**, **no te despiertes**.

Indirect Commands

The commands discussed up to this point are direct commands: A addresses B directly and indicates what B is to do. Spanish also has so-called indirect commands, in which A indicates his or her wishes by talking about B in the third person. These are usually more or less equivalent to English expressions involving "have (someone do something)" or "let (someone do something)"—*let* as in "let there be light," not *let* in the sense of permit or allow. In Spanish indirect commands are expressed by the present subjunctive, usually preceded by **que**.

Yo no quiero hacerlo. ¡Que lo haga Jorge!
I don't want to do it. Let George do it. (Have George do it.)

¿Ya han llegado? ¡Que pasen en seguida!
They've arrived already? Have them come in right away.

Rather than expressing commands, some of these constructions express wishes, very much like the wishes we sometimes express in English by an actual or implied *may*.

¿Vas al cine? ¡Que te diviertas!
You're going to the movies? Have a good time! (May you enjoy yourself!)

¿Está enferma? ¡Que se mejore!
She's sick? I hope she gets to feeling better! (May she improve!)

Some of these "wishes," primarily in certain set expressions, are not preceded by **que**.

¡Viva el emperador!
Long live the emperor!

Lo que menos quiero es criticar a mi cuñada. ¡Dios me libre!
The last thing I want to do is criticize my sister-in-law. Heaven forbid! (May God deliver me from it.)

¡Dios se lo pague!
May God reward you for it.

Most English speakers probably do not think of the concept *let's* as a command, but it is so regarded in a number of other languages, including Spanish to some extent. *Let's* can be expressed in two different ways in Spanish, by **vamos a** plus an infinitive or by a verb in the first person plural of the present subjunctive: **vamos a hablar** or **hablemos** *(let's speak)*. Note, however, that the negative "let's *not*" can be expressed only by the subjunctive: **no hablemos** *(let's not speak!)*, not **no vamos a hablar** which means *we're not going to speak*. A *let's* subjunctive form loses its final **s** when it is followed by either **nos** or **se**: **sentémonos, démoselo**.

• EXERCISE A

Change the following sentences to affirmative, then negative, familiar singular commands.

Example:
Juan se lava las manos.

Juan, lávate las manos.
Juan, no te laves las manos.

1. María pone los libros en la mesa.
2. Jorge le dice la verdad.
3. Pedro se sabe los verbos de memoria.
4. Paco me trae el coche.
5. Gloria le pide el dinero.

• EXERCISE B

Change the following sentences to affirmative, then negative, formal singular commands.

Example:
El profesor le responde en seguida.

Profesor, respóndale en seguida.
Profesor, no le responda en seguida.

1. La señora González se niega a participar.
2. Don Pedro llega bien temprano.

3. Doña Concepción se pone los guantes blancos.
4. El señor presidente se sienta aquí.
5. El licenciado Torres se divierte en la fiesta.

• EXERCISE C

Change the following sentences to affirmative, then negative, familiar plural commands.

> Example:
> Los chicos me prestan las revistas.
>
> Chicos, prestadme las revistas.
> Chicos, no me prestéis las revistas.

1. Los niños desayunan primero.
2. Contestan el teléfono.
3. Carlos y Pepita se levantan a las siete.
4. Felipe y Roberto se hacen los tontos.
5. Los alumnos se esfuerzan en aprender la lección.

• EXERCISE D

Change the following sentences to affirmative, then negative, formal plural commands.

> Example:
> Las señoras se ponen a trabajar.
>
> Señoras, pónganse a trabajar.
> Señoras, no se pongan a trabajar.

1. Los señores se quitan el sombrero.
2. Los tíos le compran un regalo.
3. Irene y Francisca se lo devuelven mañana.
4. Chavita y Marta le sirven la comida.
5. Los compañeros se van rápidamente.

• EXERCISE E

Translate the following sentences.

1. Please be careful when you open the door. (polite—singular)
2. Let's not tell them anything yet.
3. Don't buy those books. Take them out of the library.
   (familiar—singular)
4. Take off your coat, sit down, and make yourself comfortable.
   (polite—plural)
5. Let's go to the movies tonight. You find out what is showing, and then call and
   tell me. (familiar—singular)
6. Please do your assignment (**deberes**) right this time. Read the explanation
   carefully, and then complete the exercises. (polite—plural)
7. Children, please take your seats and wait quietly for your teacher to arrive.
   (familiar—plural)
8. Don't waste your time reading that junk. Use it (your time) wisely.
   (familiar—singular)
9. Write to them immediately, and then cross your fingers and wait for a
   response. (polite—singular)
10. Let's sing that one again. You give us the notes, and we will try to follow
    you. (familiar—singular)

• EXERCISE F

Using the cue provided, answer the following questions with an indirect command.

> Example:
> ¿Quién me va a llevar al centro? (Jorge)
> Que te lleve Jorge.

1. ¿Quién baila con la abuela? (el tío Ernesto)
2. ¿Quién lava los platos después de la comida? (Carlos)
3. ¿Quién le va a pedir el dinero a papá? (tu hermano)
4. ¿Quiénes van a traer el tocadiscos? (Marilú y Paquita)
5. ¿Quién paga la cuenta? (Roberto)
6. ¿Quiénes escriben todos esos ejercicios? (los alumnos)
7. ¿Quién le va a hacer la pregunta al profesor? (Marcos)
8. ¿Quién le va a decir que necesita operarse? (el doctor)
9. ¿Quién va a pasar a buscar a las chicas? (Manuel)
10. ¿A quiénes les toca llevar la cerveza? (Ricardo y Pilar)

• **EXERCISE G**

Answer the following questions using a command in your response.

1. ¿Quiere Ud. que le muestre las fotos que saqué?
2. ¿Le contamos a Ud. lo que nos ocurrió anoche?
3. ¿Jugamos al tenis o al ping pong esta tarde?
4. ¿Quién le va a escribir la carta a Carlos?
5. ¿Te traigo el libro que me regalaron?
6. ¿Les ayudamos a Uds. con esos ejercicios?
7. ¿Quieres que te haga más preguntas?
8. ¿Nos levantamos temprano mañana?
9. ¿Vamos al cine esta noche?
10. ¿Nos tenemos que acordar de todo esto?

• **EXERCISE H**

Think of five things you would really like to have. Imagine that you have the power to demand those things, and request them using a command.

Example:
Estimado profesor, póngame una "A" en el próximo examen.

9

"Probability" Expressions

Sentences can occasionally be given a flavor of conjecture or speculation or probability by the use of certain verb tenses even in English. If there is a knock at the door and I say, "Oh, that will be Roger," I am essentially saying that it "probably is" Roger. If I am told that Stanley was at the dance last night in the company of a short, blonde woman with glasses and I say, "That would be his cousin Emily," I am in effect saying that it "probably was" his cousin. This sort of usage, which is comparatively rare in English, occurs very frequently in Spanish. The following are the commonest possibilities:

1. If the verb of the "plain" sentence is in the present, the verb of the "probability" sentence is in the future.

Está enferma
She is sick.

Estará enferma.
She probably is sick. (She must be sick. I guess she's sick.)

2. If the verb of the "plain" sentence is in the imperfect, the verb of the "probability" sentence is in the conditional.

Eran las once.
It was eleven o'clock.

Serían las once.
It probably was eleven o'clock. (It must have been eleven o'clock.
I imagine it was eleven o'clock.)

3. If the verb of the "plain" sentence is in either the preterit or the present perfect, the verb of the "probability" sentence is in the future perfect.

Se vieron en la playa.
They saw each other at the beach.

Se han visto en la playa.
They have seen each other at the beach.

Se habrán visto en la playa.
They probably saw each other at the beach. (They probably have
seen each other at the beach.)

4. If the verb of the "plain" sentence is in the past perfect, the verb of the "probability" sentence is in the conditional perfect.

Lo habían leído ya.
They had already read it.

Lo habrían leído ya.
They probably had already read it. (I imagine they had already
read it.)

Note that there is no way to express "probability" by means of special verb tenses when the verb of the "plain" sentence is already in the future or conditional. In other words, the Spanish future covers "it will be so" and "it probably is so," but it cannot cover "it probably will be so"; the Spanish conditional covers "would be" and "probably was," but not "probably would be."

None of the foregoing is intended to suggest that the use of special verb tenses is the only way to express any kind of speculation or conjecture or probability in Spanish.

Julia siempre se viste de negro. Debe (de) estar de luto.
Julia always dresses in black. She must be in mourning.

Es probable que lleguen antes de las cinco.
They'll probably get here before five.

Me pregunto si ese joven es su hermano.
I wonder if that young man is his brother.

• EXERCISE A

Rewrite the following sentences using the future or conditional of probability as appropriate.

1. Debe (de) estar muy cansado después de tanto correr.
2. Me pregunto si sabe lo que está diciendo.
3. Probablemente se fueron más temprano.
4. Era probable que tuvieran mucho dinero.
5. Debe (de) haber estudiado mucho para sacar esa nota.
6. Tú probablemente nunca me has oído tocar el piano.
7. Me pregunto dónde dejé las llaves del auto.
8. El probablemente ha crecido mucho en tu ausencia.
9. Me parece probable que se haya olvidado de ti.
10. Juan probablemente se lastimó *(hurt himself)* jugando al fútbol.
11. María Luisa debió (de) estar fantástica anoche.
12. Probablemente ya se lo había dicho.
13. ¿Te parece que han preparado bien la lección?
14. Eran probablemente las cinco de la mañana cuando llegó.
15. El probablemente estaba tan contento que no se dio cuenta de la hora que era.

• EXERCISE B

Translate the following sentences to present orally in class.

1. I asked you because I thought you probably knew, not to embarrass you.
2. I wonder where that darn book is. Whenever I need it, it disappears.
3. Don't bother to call now; I think they've probably already left.
4. How do you suppose he could say such a ridiculous thing (**disparate**) when he knows it isn't true and never could be?
5. The lady can't say for sure, but she assumes that it must have been late, that they probably were tired, and that it must have been just a momentary slip on their part that permitted it to happen.
6. They must have been waiting about three hours already, and it still has not stopped raining.
7. I guess he was feeling remorseful or I don't know what; anyway, he went back to the store and returned what he had taken.

8. With everything you told him, by this time he must be madder than the devil.
9. What do you suppose he was thinking about to show up in that condition in the chamber of deputies? It's that the poor man has had a lot of problems for years.
10. I've been looking for it everywhere for an hour, and I can't find it. I probably threw it out without realizing it.
11. It's useless for you to do it now. By this time they will have turned it in.
12. That guy must be crazy! Just imagine speaking to a policeman that way.
13. He was probably very tired; if not, he would have corrected it already.
14. I can't tell exactly, but he must be forty years old, more or less.
15. You must have studied a lot to come out so well on that exam.

• EXERCISE C

To make sure it is clear to you to which "plain" tenses the various "probability" tenses are related, change each of the following sentences to *remove* any element of speculation, conjecture, or probability.

> Example:
> Serían las tres cuando llegamos.
> Eran las tres cuando llegamos.
>
> Julián habrá vendido su coche.
> Julián vendió (*or* ha vendido) su coche.

1. Arnulfo no habla en la clase. Le tendrá miedo al profesor.
2. Alguien está llamando a la puerta. ¿Quién será?
3. Gloria tendría unos veinte años cuando se casó.
4. ¿Quién le habrá contado a Salvador lo que pasó?
5. Rosita no fue al baile. Estaría enferma.
6. La pera había desaparecido. Se la habría comido Consuelo.
7. ¿Será verdad lo que nos contaron?
8. Lo siento, pero yo no soy el autor de *Cien años de soledad.* Ud. se habrá equivocado.
9. Hoy tocaron bastante mal. Estarían muy cansados.
10. Parece que José Luis quiere entrar pero no puede. Se le habrá perdido la llave.

• EXERCISE D

Translate the following sentences.

1. I supposed that they would have given him all the details of your little escapade.

2. Who could have given her all that money? Yesterday she didn't even have a dollar.
3. What time must it have been when the accident occurred?
4. It must have been about three in the morning, unless I'm mistaken.
5. I know I have seen you somewhere. We must have met in some Spanish class.
6. Do you suppose the party is over? It's barely two in the morning.
7. It was probably Charles who told him about last night because he was the only one who returned early.
8. The water must be very cold. If not, they would have been in it already.
9. He must have been very happy with his new conquest because we didn't see him again all night.
10. Do you think that we have arrived? I can't see or hear a thing, but the train has stopped.
11. I'm not sure, but it's probably nine o'clock already. No wonder you are so hungry.
12. How stupid can I be! I completely forgot that today is your birthday.
13. If he told you not to do it, he probably had his reasons. In any case, it's too late now.
14. Where are the keys? They must be there in your room where you left them.
15. I wonder how I came out on that test last night? You probably got an "A" as always.

• EXERCISE E

Answer the following questions in Spanish.

1. Algunos de los alumnos están ausentes. ¿Se habrán olvidado de que hay clase hoy?
2. ¿Qué hora sería cuando Ud. llegó a su primera clase esta mañana?
3. ¿En qué parte del mundo se habrá inventado la rueda?
4. ¿Qué edad tendría Shakespeare cuando escribió *Romeo y Julieta*?
5. ¿Estará nevando en este momento en el Polo Norte?
6. ¿Serán peligrosos los gorilas?
7. ¿Estará aburrido el profesor de esta clase?
8. Un gran admirador del actor Clark Gable no fue a ver *Lo que el viento se llevó*. ¿Lo habría visto antes, o no tendría dinero para pagar la entrada?
9. ¿Cuántos granos habrá en un metro cúbico de arena?
10. ¿Cuántos ejemplares se habrán publicado ya de *Alicia en el país de las maravillas*?

• EXERCISE F

Read the following paragraph carefully. Identify all "probability" expressions and explain their use.

Alguien llama a la puerta. ¿Quién será? ¿Podrá ser Rosario? Y si es ella, ¿por qué vendrá a verme? ¿Se habrá enterado *(found out)* de que fui al baile con su novio? Creo que él se llama Enrique. Sí, Enrique. Y si se ha enterado ¿estará bien enojada conmigo? No sé. Después de todo, ésa no será la primera vez que Enrique ha salido con otra. Y no estará tan enamorada de él que... Ya voy, ya voy... ¡Enrique! ¿Será Enrique? Ojalá que no. ¿Por qué me habrá invitado al baile? ¿Estaría enojado con Rosario? ¿O estará ya un poco cansado de ella? Eso se entendería. Pero ¿por qué habrá venido ahora? Seguramente no me habré olvidado de decirle que no podemos seguir viéndonos, al fin y al cabo Rosario es mi mejor amiga, y en todo caso, yo estoy comprometida con... ¡Ay Dios mío, Ricardo! Debe ser Ricardo. Pero ¿cómo habrá sabido él que...? Y con lo celoso que es! ¿Qué diablos voy a hacer ahora? . . . ¡Está bien, está bien, ya voy! . . . Será mejor que me entere ya de una vez quién llama a ésa puerta. ¡Hola! ¡Pero muy buenas tardes! ¡Qué bueno que hayas venido! Precisamente en este momento estaba pensando . . . .

Now write a one-page composition based on the above, but pretend you are either Rosario, Enrique, or Ricardo. Try to use as many "probability" expressions as you legitimately can.

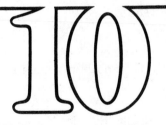

Hacer
in Time
Expressions

The following are the usual possibilities for using **hacer** in time expressions.

1. **Hace** plus a verb in the present tense tells how long something has been going on as of now.

> Hace tres años que viven en Copenhague.
> *They have lived in Copenhagen for three years.*

2. **Hacía** plus a verb in the imperfect tells how long something had been going on as of some past time.

> Hacía tres años que vivían en Copenhague (cuando yo los conocí).
> *They had been living in Copenhagen for three years (when I met them).*

3. **Hace** plus a verb in a past tense (preterit or imperfect depending on the context) tells how long ago something happened (with relation to the present).

> Hace tres años vivían en Copenhague.
> *Three years ago they were living in Copenhagen.*

Hace tres años hicieron un viaje a Copenhague.
Three years ago they took a trip to Copenhagen.

4. **Hacía** plus a verb in the past perfect tells how much earlier something had happened (with relation to some past time).

Hacía tres años habían hecho un viaje a Copenhague.
Three years before (three years earlier) they had taken a trip to Copenhagen.

When an **hacer** expression of the "how long has (or had) it been going on" type begins the sentence, the following part of the sentence is normally introduced by **que**.

Hace muchos años que tengo estos problemas.
I've had these problems for many years.

However, **hacer** expressions of the "how long ago" type can occur both with and without **que**, usually with a slight difference in emphasis.

Hace dos meses se le murió el abuelo.
His grandfather died two months ago.
(What happened two months ago? Two months ago his grandfather died.)

Hace dos meses que se le murió el abuelo.
His grandfather died two months ago.
(How long ago did his grandfather die? His grandfather died two months ago.)

When **hacer** expressions of the "how long has (had) it been going on" type follow the other part of the sentence, they are usually (though not always) preceded by **desde**. Expressions of the "ago" type are not.

Lo conozco desde hace dos meses.
I've known him for two months.

Lo conocí hace dos meses.
I met him two months ago.

Left to his own devices, an English speaker would probably translate the sentence "I have lived in Madrid five years" as "He vivido en Madrid cinco años." As a matter of fact, this construction does exist in Spanish and in some regions is not uncommon. However, it is still advisable for an English-speaking student of Spanish to learn the **hacer** construction described above since in the greater part of the Spanish-speaking world this is the normal way to express how long something has been going on.

• EXERCISE A

Complete the following sentences.

1. _____ dos años que _____ español.
   I have been studying Spanish for two years.
2. _____ veinte minutos que te _____ .
   She has been waiting for you for twenty minutes.
3. _____ sólo seis meses que los _____ .
   We have only known them for six months.
4. _____ siete semanas que _____ aquí cuando lo supo.
   She had been working here for seven weeks when she heard about it.
5. _____ años que se lo _____ , pero no te creyó.
   You had been telling him that for years, but he wouldn't believe you.
6. ¿Cuántos años _____ que nos _____ ?
   How many years ago was it that we first met?
7. Me _____ a su casa _____ tres semanas.
   He invited me to his house three weeks ago.
8. _____ quince años que no _____ a la Argentina.
   I had not been back to Argentina for fifteen years.
9. Te _____ eso _____ un minuto.
   I told you that a minute ago.
10. _____ desde _____ dos horas.
    He has been crying for two hours.

• EXERCISE B

Answer the following questions according to the clues given.

1. ¿Cuánto tiempo hace que María habla por teléfono? (dos horas)
2. ¿Desde cuándo has estado ahí sentado? (veinte minutos)
3. ¿Cuánto tiempo hacía que no ganábamos un partido? (tres años)
4. ¿Desde cuándo se escriben Carlota y Roberto? (cinco meses)
5. ¿Cuándo viste a Jorge por última vez? (hace cuatro años)
6. ¿Cuántos años hacía que no bailabas el tango? (quince)

7. ¿Cuánto hace que recibieron la noticia? (tres horas)
8. ¿Desde cuándo no sales con María Luisa? (dos semanas)
9. ¿Cuándo vivían ustedes en Montevideo? (hace siete años)
10. ¿Hace cuánto (que) llegó Ud. a esta ciudad? (un mes)

• EXERCISE C

Translate the following sentences to present orally in class.

1. I hadn't heard that song for years, but when I heard him sing it, tears came (form of **saltar**) to my eyes.
2. I returned from Japan about twenty years ago, but I still remember the beauty of its landscapes.
3. I've been studying Portuguese for four years, and it's still hard for me.
4. We had only been talking a few minutes when he suddenly withdrew without saying a word.
5. I've had that project finished since last week, and now he says it's not to be turned in.
6. I have been wanting to talk to you for an hour, but there was always someone who prevented it.
7. We had been preparing for that occasion for eight weeks, which became obvious when we saw the results we obtained.
8. I told you to bring it to me half an hour ago, and I simply cannot wait any longer.
9. I've been in Madrid since June, and I can't get them to give me permission to leave.
10. At that time I hadn't participated in such performances (**funciones**) for months; nevertheless, a few minutes after beginning I felt completely comfortable in the role I was playing.

• EXERCISE D

Translate the following sentences.

1. Years ago I heard that expression from (in) the mouth of a Chilean friend, but since then I hadn't heard it again until you used it a moment ago.
2. They've been on the road (**de camino**) for days, but they can't succeed in getting to their destination because their car keeps breaking down.
3. Three years ago, while I was in Tangier, I fell under the influence of her charms, and I haven't been able to free myself of them till the present.
4. This can't be tolerated any longer; he took them the manuscript more than two weeks ago and they still haven't made (form of **sacar**) him the necessary copies.

5. Three months went by from his arrival in this country until he got in touch with me. Now for two weeks he hasn't failed to call me even a single day.
6. How long had you been waiting when they arrived? I don't know exactly, but it seemed like an eternity.
7. Since what day have you gone without (form of **estar sin**) eating? Man, if you don't take care of yourself, you're going to end up lighter than a feather **(quedar hecho una pluma)**.
8. He hadn't felt that good for a long time. Obviously your support was indispensable to him.
9. The performance had only been going on for a few minutes when the film broke.
10. That guy **(tipo)** has been a constant nuisance to me since the day on which he appeared around here with his pedantic bragging and his ceaseless talking.

• EXERCISE E

Answer the following questions in Spanish.

1. ¿Sabe Ud. cuánto tiempo hacía que sus padres se conocían cuando se casaron?
2. ¿Cuál era el medio de transporte más importante hace quinientos años?
3. ¿Cuánto tiempo hace que Ud. empezó a estudiar español?
4. ¿Hacía mucho tiempo que tenía Ud. ganas de aprender el español cuando empezó a estudiarlo?
5. ¿Dónde vivía Ud. hace diez años?
6. ¿Recuerda Ud. cuánto tiempo hace que vio una jirafa por primera vez?
7. ¿Cuánto tiempo hace que se publicó el libro que estamos usando en esta clase?
8. ¿Todavía había dinosaurios hace diez mil años?
9. Si Ud. en este momento tiene hambre o sed, ¿cuánto tiempo hace que la tiene?
10. ¿Cuántos años hace que aprendió Ud. a manejar?

• EXERCISE F

Read the following paragraphs carefully, paying special attention to the time expressions.

El señor Jones ha estado en este país desde 1963. Es decir, que hace ya quince años que vive en un país de habla española, y todavía no consigue expresarse claramente. Además, antes de llegar aquí, hacía años que estudiaba el español con un profesor privado, pero sin resultado alguno. Cada vez que abría la boca salían unos sonidos bárbaros que parecían ser de otro mundo, ya que no pertenecían a ningún sistema conocido hasta el momento.

Yo lo conocí hace mes y medio, cuando me encontraba en la jefatura *(headquarters)* de la policía tratando de ver a un cliente mío que había tenido unos problemas unos días antes. Hacía dos semanas que tenían preso al pobre Jones porque no conseguía aclarar un enredo *(tangle)* que había resultado de su incapacidad de comunicación. Después de interceder por él con un amigo que tengo en el gobierno, logramos que lo pusieran en libertad. Desde ese día el señor Jones está más decidido que nunca a aprender a hablar español. Hace unos días me crucé con él en la calle, y después de lo que pareció una eternidad, creí entenderle algo como, "Buenas tardes, licenciado Pérez."

Now write a similar paragraph or two in which you try to use many different time expressions.

11

Personal Pronouns

The term *personal pronouns* refers to words such as *them, I, us, you, it, we,* or *her*. In Spanish these words can have different forms depending on whether they are used as (1) the subject of a verb, (2) the direct object of a verb, (3) the indirect object of a verb, or (4) the object of a preposition, although no one pronoun has separate forms for all four of these uses.

Verbs often report things that someone (or something) does. Some of these are things that are simply done ("He walked across the room"), but others are things that are done *to* someone (or something)—"I saw John" or "The lion attacked the gazelle." The person or thing on which the action expressed by the verb is performed is usually called the *direct object* of the verb. In "I saw John," *John* is the direct object of *saw* since John is the person I saw; in "The lion attacked the gazelle," *gazelle* is the direct object of *attacked* since the gazelle is what the lion attacked.

In addition to the direct object, a sentence may also contain a so-called indirect object, a person or thing who does not actually receive the brunt of the action but is still involved or affected in some way. In "Helen gives Roger the money," the money is what Helen really gives, and *money* is therefore the direct object of *gives;* however, Roger is certainly involved, inasmuch as he gets the money, and *Roger* is said to be the indirect object of *gives.*

The distinction just described is not usually a problem in dealing with Spanish **me, te, nos, os,** and **se** since all of these pronouns can be used as either direct or indirect objects.

> Me (te, nos, etc.) miraron.
> *They looked at me (you, us, etc.)*
> (Direct object.)

> Me (te, nos, etc.) regalaron un globo.
> *They gave me (you, us, etc.) a balloon.*
> (Indirect object.)

However, in order to use **lo, la, le, los, las,** and **les** correctly one must differentiate between a direct and an indirect object.

> Lo vimos.
> *We saw him.*
> (Direct object.)

> Le explicamos el problema.
> *We explained the problem to him.*
> (Indirect object.)

> Las visité.
> *I visited them.*
> (Direct object.)

> Les dije la verdad.
> *I told them the truth.*
> (Indirect object.)

Officially, the third-person direct object pronouns in Spanish are **lo, la, los,** and **las;** indirect objects are **le** and **les,** and there is really no valid reason for English-speaking students of Spanish not to conform to this usage. At the same time, however, English speakers should not be shocked if they encounter examples of both *laísmo* and *leísmo. Laísmo* is the tendency (in Spain) to use **la** and **las** as feminine indirect object pronouns. *Leísmo* is the tendency (in Spain and to a limited extent in Latin America) to use **le** and **les** as masculine direct object pronouns, especially when referring to people.

La vi y la di el dinero.
Instead of: La vi y le di el dinero.
I saw her and I gave the money to her.
(Laísmo.)

Le vi y le di el dinero.
Instead of: Lo vi y le di el dinero.
I saw him and I gave the money to him.
(Leísmo.)

In English (and for the most part in Spanish), the indirect object is usually understood as a *to* or *for* concept, even though the actual *to* or *for* may only be implied in the English sentence.

Les hicimos un favor.
We did them a favor. (We did a favor for *them.)*

Le conté una historia espeluznante.
I told him a hair-raising story. (I told a hair-raising story to *him.)*

In Spanish, however, an indirect object is also used with several common verbs to express a *from* relationship.

Les robamos un reloj.
We stole a watch from *them.*

Le compré un escritorio.
I bought a desk from *her.*
(This can also mean, depending on the context, that I bought
a desk *for* her.)

Les quitaron los documentos.
They took their papers away from *them.*

Le pidieron dinero.
They asked him for money. (They requested money from *him.)*

A number of verbs that take a direct object in English take an indirect object in Spanish. The following are a few of the more common ones: **pegar** *to hit,* **ganar** *to beat (someone at something),* **interesar** *to interest,* **creer** *to believe a person (to believe a thing* takes a direct object), **servir** *to serve a person (to serve a thing* takes a direct object), **gustar** *to please.* The following examples are set up in terms of "her" in order to call attention to the indirect objects.

Nadie le creyó.
Nobody believed her.
(*But:* Nadie lo creyó. *Nobody believed it.*)

No le interesaron nada las cosas que le contamos.
The things we told her didn't interest her at all.

¿Por qué no le gustó?
Why didn't she like it? (Why didn't it please her?)

It is very common for a noun *indirect* object to be repeated by a pronoun indirect object that to an English speaker may seem unnecessary.

Le di el libro a Jorge.
I gave the book to Jorge.
(**Jorge** and **le** refer to the same person. They are *indirect* objects.)

Do not get carried away with this construction and try to apply it to noun *direct* objects also.

Vi a Jorge.
I saw Jorge.
(Not "Lo vi a Jorge" although this construction can be found in colloquial speech in some parts of the Spanish-speaking world.
Here there is no pronoun object because **Jorge** is a *direct* object.)

Any noun object, direct or indirect, however, tends to be repeated by a pronoun object *when it precedes the verb.* This should be regarded as a rule different and separate from the preceding one.

A Jorge lo veo todos los días, mientras que a Pedro no lo veo más que los domingos.
Jorge I see every day, while Pedro I only see on Sundays.
(Direct objects.)

A Jorge le di cien dólares, pero a Pedro le di quinientos.
To Jorge I gave a hundred dollars, but to Pedro I gave five hundred.
(Indirect objects.)

A few common verbs, especially **decir** and to a considerable extent **preguntar** and **saber,** are frequently used with a direct object **lo** in situations in which there would be no *it* in the corresponding English sentence.

Nos lo preguntaron, pero no lo sabíamos.
They asked us, but we didn't know. (They asked it of us, but we didn't know it.)

Le pregunté si era alemana, pero no quiso decírmelo.
I asked her if she was German, but she wouldn't tell me.
(She wouldn't tell it to me.)

In English, and for the most part in Spanish, an object pronoun is used to replace the direct or indirect object of a verb. However, in Spanish, unlike English, a predicate noun ("Henry is a *teacher*") or a predicate adjective ("Julia is *intelligent*") can also be replaced by a pronoun. The pronoun in this construction is always **lo**; it does not agree with the noun involved.

Mis tías son ricas, pero mis hermanas no lo son.
My aunts are rich, but my sisters aren't.

In earlier Spanish (and to a limited extent still today, in formal literary style) object pronouns can be found attached to almost any verb form.

Diríase que no es ésta la hija del rey.
It would appear that this is not the daughter of the king.

In contemporary Spanish, however, object pronouns are for all practical purposes attached only to the following three kinds of verb forms.

1. Affirmative commands.
Diles la verdad.
Tell them the truth.
(Object pronouns *precede* negative commands. [No les digas la verdad. *Don't tell them the truth.*])

2. Infinitives.
Darle el dinero ahora sería poco aconsejable.
To give her the money now wouldn't be very advisable.

3. Present participles (**-ndo** forms; in Spanish, **gerundios**).
El subjuntivo lo aprenderás estudiándolo.
You will learn the subjunctive by studying it.

If an infinitive or **-ndo** form is preceded by another verb, the object pronoun can, in most cases, be placed in front of the first verb.

Quiere comprarlo.   Lo quiere comprar.
He wants to buy it.

Está leyéndola.   La está leyendo.
He's reading it.

When two object pronouns are used with the same verb, the general rule to follow is that the indirect object precedes the direct.

Admiré su collar y me lo regaló.
I admired her necklace and she gave it (direct object) *to me*
(indirect object).

Whatever its function, however, **se** always precedes any other object pronoun.

Se me olvidó que no sabía inglés.
I forgot that he didn't know English.
(Literally, it forgot itself [direct object] to me [indirect object] that
he didn't know English.)

Furthermore, pairs of object pronouns (**me los, nos la, te los**, etc.) consisting of an indirect object followed by a direct object can be used only when the direct object is **lo, la, los,** or **las.**

Me la presentaron.
They introduced her (direct object) *to me* (indirect object).

Sentences in which the direct object in such a pair is **me, te, nos,** or **os** must use the following construction.

Me presentaron a ella.
They introduced me (direct object) *to her* (indirect object).

If applying the rule "indirect object precedes direct object" would result in a pair of object pronouns both beginning with an **l,** the first pronoun in the pair (which will be either **le** or **les**) is replaced by **se.**

Me pidieron dinero y se lo di.
They asked me for money and I gave it to them.

It should be noted that the **se** of this construction has a totally different historical origin from the reflexive **se** (meaning *oneself*) and should not be confused with the reflexive **se.**

Pairs of object pronouns are placed either before or after various verb forms in accordance with the rules indicated above for the placement of single object pronouns.

Nos mira. *But:* ¡Míranos! (Affirmative command.)
Quiere mirarnos. (Infinitive.)
Está mirándonos. (Present participle.)

Nos lo da. *But:* ¡Dánoslo! (Affirmative command.)
Quiere dárnoslo. (Infinitive.)
Está dándonoslo. (Present participle.)

In English, almost any word can be emphasized by giving it greater stress or prominence, whereas in Spanish there are certain words, among them the object pronouns under discussion here, that are simply not "stressable." In other words, while it is possible in English to say "it seems to *me* that . . . ," it is not possible to say in Spanish "*me* parece que . . . ." In such situations, Spanish uses, *in addition to* the object pronouns that immediately precede or follow the verb, phrases such as **a mí, a él, a nosotros,** or **a ustedes.**

A ellos no les gusta nada.
They *don't* like it at all.

Sometimes these added phrases are also needed to clarify a sentence that would be confusing or ambiguous without them.

No tengo inconveniente en decírselo a usted, pero no quiero
decírselo a él.
I don't mind telling you, but I don't want to tell him.

However, when English speakers find out about these "emphatic" or "clarifying" phrases, they sometimes have a tendency to overuse them. It is true that a phrase like **se los** can, depending on the circumstances, mean *them to her, them to him, them to you,* or *them to them,* but in practice it is usually clear from the context who is meant.

The only distinctive forms that exist for use after prepositions are **mí, ti,** and the reflexive **sí** (meaning *himself, herself, itself, themselves, yourself,* or *yourselves*). Note that **mí** and **sí** have written accents (to distinguish them from the possessive **mi** *my* and **si** *if*) but **ti** does not. Note also the forms **conmigo, contigo,** and **consigo.** Otherwise the same pronouns are used after prepositions as are used as subjects (**para usted, con él, a nosotros**). In many parts of the Spanish-speaking world, the nonreflexive pronouns are also used colloquially instead of the reflexives (**para ella** instead of **para sí, con él** instead of **consigo**).

• EXERCISE A

Answer the following questions using pronouns in place of noun objects.

1. ¿Me trajiste el libro que te pedí?
2. ¿Escribiste la tarjeta para María?
3. ¿Nos dijeron la verdad?
4. ¿Conoces a la chica de azul?
5. ¿Te contaron lo que nos ocurrió anoche?
6. ¿Se ha quitado el sombrero el profesor?
7. ¿Le ganaron las figuritas que querían?
8. ¿Le creyeron lo que les dijo Rafael?
9. ¿Les permite cantar en español?
10. ¿Le llevo el café a papá?

• EXERCISE B

Complete the following sentences as indicated.

1. _____ pedí a Ricardo que _____ trajera, pero no quiso hacer_____ .
   I asked Richard to bring it (the car) to me, but he didn't want to do it.
2. _____ escribimos el mes pasado, y todavía no _____ han contestado.
   We wrote to them last month, and they still have not answered us.
3. Permíte_____ que _____ enseñe la poesía. _____ escribió anoche.
   Allow him to show you the poem. He wrote it last night.
4. _____ digo para que _____ enteres de lo que en realidad está ocurriendo.
   I'm telling you so you will find out what is really happening.
5. A Roberto _____ encuentro cada dos o tres días, pero a Carlota hace meses
   que no _____ veo.
   I run into Robert every two or three days, but Carlota I haven't seen in months.
6. No _____ creímos cuando _____ dijo que _____ había ganado en ese juego.
   We didn't believe him when he told us he had beaten her in that game.
7. _____ dijo porque estaba convencida de que _____ convendría saber_____ .
   *She told us because she was convinced that it would profit us to
   know it.*
8. A María no _____ gusta que nadie _____ moleste.
   Mary does not like anybody to bother her.
9. Yo _____ dije a esa señora, así que no _____ venga a decir que
   no _____ sabían.
   I told it to that lady, so don't come around saying that they didn't know it.

10. A usted ya _____ pregunté, a Marta _____ quiero ver en mi oficina inmediatamente, y a los demás _____ hablaré mañana.
I already asked you, I want to see Marta in my office immediately, and I will talk to the rest of you tomorrow.

• EXERCISE C

Translate the following sentences to present orally in class.

1. If you hadn't told me, there's no way I would have known it.
2. The fact that you are telling me about it now is inconsequential. I ought to have known it yesterday when it was important.
3. If you don't know, ask the gentleman who is in charge of the session.
4. Nobody believed him until he showed us the documentation.
5. He asked us to stick it (the picture) to the back of the sheet.
6. Don't hit the dog if you don't want him to bite you.
7. Pay them what they are asking, and let's quit messing around (**dejémonos de cuentos**).
8. When they bring you the bill, pay it. We will wait for you in the car.
9. May it benefit (form of **aprovechar**) you!
10. How could he find out about the results so soon? Somebody had to tell him. I told him.

• EXERCISE D

Rewrite the following sentences replacing the object nouns with the corresponding pronouns.

1. Tráigame el libro de matemáticas.
2. No le cuente a Rosario lo de la fiesta.
3. Entregaron los exámenes al profesor.
4. Estaba recitando una poesía a la clase. (Two ways.)
5. Queremos mostrarles el coche a nuestros amigos. (Two ways.)
6. No les muestres esas fotos a tus compañeros.
7. Nos leyó esta lección.
8. Seguía diciéndole la verdad. (Two ways.)
9. El cartero trajo este paquete para Ud.
10. No le digan a Ricardo lo que pasó.

• EXERCISE E

Complete the following sentences as indicated.

1. Si el jefe _____ ha indicado su preferencia, conviene no contrariar_____ .
   If the boss has indicated his preference to you, you'd better not cross him.
2. Esas flores son sumamente hermosas. Tiene Ud. razón; no _____ hay más bonitas.
   Those flowers are extremely beautiful. You're right; there aren't any more beautiful.
3. El libro que _____ prestaste se _____ perdió.
   The book you lent me got lost.
4. Si no _____ quieres decir ahora, _____ espero a la salida de la clase.
   If you don't want to tell it to me now, I'll wait for you after class.
5. _____ pedí porque los míos _____ acabaron.
   I asked you for them (the cigarettes) because mine are all gone.
6. Si no _____ hubiera querido dar, _____ hubiera dicho.
   If he had not wanted to give them (the books) to us, he would have said so.
7. No _____ gusta que _____ prestes a nadie, a menos que yo _____ autorice.
   I don't like for you to lend them (the trucks) to anyone unless I authorize it.
8. _____ es imposible venir esta noche. Tal vez _____ veas mañana.
   It's impossible for them to come tonight. Perhaps you will see them tomorrow.
9. María siempre _____ sabe todo, y _____ dice cada vez que _____ veo.
   Mary always knows it all, and tells me so every time I see her.
10. No _____ compres a Juan. Yo quiero vender _____ el mío.
    Don't buy John's (the ticket). I want to sell you mine.

• EXERCISE F

Translate the following sentences.

1. They were very pleased to see you so soon.
2. You still have not brought me the articles I requested.
3. I have known her for six months, but I don't like her very much.
4. Please, Dad, buy it (the car) for me!
5. Richard I will see tomorrow, but I want to talk to you right now.
6. Don't forget to buy a doll for Susie, a ball for Todd, and if you have any money left, I would like that ring I showed you.

7. He was bringing it (the cake) to me very carefully, but he dropped it.
8. Keep mixing it (the paint) until it's all the same color.
9. Please don't lose them (the rings) for me. They cost me a fortune.
10. They took the documents from her, put her in that small room, and won't let her speak to anyone.

• EXERCISE G

Answer the following questions in Spanish.

1. ¿Dónde le gustaría más sentarse, adelante o atrás de la clase?
2. ¿Cuándo estudia Ud. su lección de español?
3. ¿Por qué trae Ud. los libros a la clase?
4. ¿Cuándo se pone Ud. un abrigo?
5. ¿Conoce Ud. a todos sus compañeros de clase?
6. ¿Le gustaría conocerlos? ¿Por qué?
7. ¿Se le ha olvidado alguna vez algo importante?
8. ¿Se ha imaginado alguna vez lo que sería ser millonario?

• EXERCISE H

Read the following letter identifying the use of all personal pronouns.

Querido Juan:

Perdóname la demora en hacerte llegar esta carta. Te la hubiera escrito antes, pero cada vez que me propuse hacerlo, me lo impedía algo que no consigo explicarme bien. Tengo plena conciencia de que las noticias que esperas te son muy importantes. Sé que sin ellas no les puedes dar la información que les prometiste a tus compañeros, sin embargo, no sabes lo que me cuesta escribirte estas palabras. Si alguien me hubiera dicho que me vería en tal circunstancia, no se lo hubiera creído. Siempre me he imaginado ser capaz de responder a cualquier situación que se me presentara. Pero te confieso que me están entrando dudas al respecto. La verdad es que se me ocurrió que una vez que empezara a escribirte esta carta, me sería más fácil llegar al grano, pero como te habrás dado cuenta, llevo ya más de media página, y todavía no te he dicho lo que te es necesario saber. Me parece que me equivoqué. Esto se me está haciendo cada vez más difícil. Sencillamente no te lo puedo decir. No te impacientes. Te prometo que la semana que viene te vuelvo a escribir, y entonces sí te lo digo todo. Hasta entonces,

tu buen amigo

Rodolfo

Now write a one-page letter to Rodolfo in which you try to get him to tell you what he finds so difficult to express, or rewrite this letter to Juan and tell him the information he has been waiting to hear. Make the letter interesting!

12

Reflexives and the Uses of Se

In its original and most literal sense, the term *reflexive* refers to a situation in which the subject does something to itself.

Me quemé.
I burned myself.

Se puso una inyección.
He gave himself an injection.

As these examples indicate, such constructions occur in both Spanish and English. In Spanish, however, a number of verbs are used reflexively to express concepts which in English are not usually viewed as reflexive and are expressed in other ways.

Levanta pesas.
He lifts weights.
Se levanta a las siete.
He gets up at seven. (He raises himself at seven.)

Acostó a los niños.
He put the children to bed.
Se acostó.
He went to bed. (He put himself to bed.)

La senté al lado de Jorge.
I seated her beside Jorge.
Me senté al lado de Jorge.
I sat down beside Jorge. (I seated myself beside Jorge.)

Despedimos a un mecanógrafo.
We dismissed (fired) a typist.
Nos despedimos de nuestros amigos.
We said good-bye to our friends.
(We dismissed ourselves from our friends.)

Sus chistes me divirtieron mucho.
His jokes amused me a great deal.
Me divertí mucho.
I had a very good time. (I amused myself a great deal.)

Su primera novela la hizo famosa.
Her first novel made her famous.
Se hizo famosa.
She became famous. (She made herself famous.)

El trabajo nos cansó.
The work tired us.
Nos cansamos.
We got tired. (We tired ourselves.)

In Spanish there are reflexive uses of even intransitive verbs, which by definition are not supposed to take a direct object of any kind, reflexive or otherwise. (It is true that a reflexive object pronoun can also be an *indirect* object, as in **se lavó la cara** *he washed his face,* but that is not the explanation for these intransitive reflexives.)

Se fue.
He left. (He went away.)

Me dormí.
I fell asleep. (I went to sleep.)

Se murieron.
They died.

La casa se vino abajo.
The house collapsed.

Se cayó.
She fell down.

A few verbs are simply always reflexive.

Se quejaron de mi conducta.
They complained about my conduct.

¿Cómo te atreviste a hacer eso?
How did you dare to do that?

Se arrepintieron de lo que habían hecho.
They regretted (repented of) what they had done.

The reflexive is the simplest and commonest way of expressing the concept "each other."

Se conocen bien.
They know each other well.

Nos escribíamos todos los días.
We were writing to each other every day.

More specific ways of saying "each other" do exist and in some situations are useful and necessary.

Coloqué los libros el uno encima del otro.
I placed the books on top of each other.

However, English speakers sometimes overwork expressions of the "uno a otro" type and would be well advised to stick to the simple reflexive for expressing "each other" whenever they can.

In English, one common device for stating that something is done, without specifying who in particular does it, is the use of indefinite, nonspecific subjects such as *people, one, you, they,* and *we*. (It is important to understand that we are talking here about a generalized, unidentified *you, we,* and *they*—not a *you, we,* or *they* that refers to anyone specific.)

People don't like being told what to do.

One doesn't do that in polite society.

I think you can get it at a health food store.
(You can get it = one can get it, people in general can get it;
not just you, the specific person I'm talking to.)

In this country we shake hands when we are introduced.
(We shake hands = people in general shake hands, everybody does.)

They say he will be the next president.
(They say = a number of unidentified people say; not *they* meaning
anybody specific.)

In addition to using indefinite, unidentified subjects, English uses the so-called
passive voice to report what happens without specifying who is responsible.

The church was built in 1895.
(Someone built it, but the sentence doesn't say who.)

Catalan is spoken in Andorra.
(The sentence doesn't specify who it is spoken by. Presumably by
people in general.)

It is believed that porpoises are more intelligent than amoebas.
(The sentence doesn't say who in particular believes it. Various
unidentified people.)

Both of these devices (nonspecific subject and passive voice) for saying what
is done without specifying who does it are found in Spanish also.

Antes que te cases, mira lo que haces.
Look before you leap.
(*You* meaning anybody, not just the particular person I'm talking to.)

Uno tiene que acostumbrarse a muchas cosas en esta sociedad.
A person has to get used to a lot of things in this society.
(Everyone has to, people in general have to.)

Dicen que va a llover.
They say it's going to rain.
(Vague, unidentified *they*.)

Esta universidad fue fundada en el siglo trece.
This university was founded in the thirteenth century.
(But the sentence doesn't specify who it was founded by.)

In addition to using indefinite subjects and passive voice, there exists a third way of reporting what is done without saying who does it: the reflexive construction. In other words, instead of saying that X does something to Y, it is said (although this is not to be taken literally) that Y does whatever it is to itself. This device is rarely used in English but in Spanish is very common, probably more common than either of the other two previously mentioned devices.

¿Qué se come con bacalao?
What is eaten with codfish? (What does one eat with codfish?
What do people eat with codfish?)

En Burdeos se habla francés.
French is spoken in Bordeaux. (In Bordeaux they speak French.
[Indefinite, unidentified *they.*] *In Bordeaux people speak French.)*

Se supone que son italianos.
It is assumed that they are Italians.
(We assume that they are Italians. [Generalized, nonspecific *we.*]
People assume that they are Italians.)

El libro se publicó en 1964.
The book was published in 1964.
(Somebody unidentified published it.)

In talking about people rather than things, this construction could conceivably produce ambiguous statements, since people really can perform actions on themselves in ways that things cannot, and so has traditionally been avoided. In contemporary colloquial Spanish, however, this construction's use with reference to people is fairly common.

El general se mató en la batalla.
The general was killed in the battle.
(Unless otherwise specified, this would not usually mean that the general literally killed himself [committed suicide] during the battle.)

Note the verb form in the following example.

Aquí se venden libros.
Books are sold here.

This sentence is literally supposed to mean that books sell themselves here, which implies that *they* sell themselves here, and so the verb appears in the *they* form (third person plural). Traditionally this has been considered the only "correct" version of such a sentence. However, in contemporary colloquial usage, **se**, while continuing to observe the rules of word order applicable to a reflexive object pronoun, has in meaning become very nearly equivalent to a sort of nonspecific, unidentified subject pronoun similar to French *on,* German *man,* and (formal and British) English *one.* It is not uncommon, therefore, to encounter not only the officially approved "aquí se venden libros" but also "aquí se vende libros" with the verb (**vende**) in the singular even though the noun that is supposed to be its subject (**libros**) is in the plural.

Note that **se** cannot be used to mean *one* if it is already needed as the object of a reflexive verb.

> Todo empieza mal cuando uno se levanta temprano.
> *Everything starts out badly when one gets up early.*

• EXERCISE A

Complete the following sentences as indicated.

1. _____ en una situación algo complicada en estos días, por lo cual no _____ hablar en público.
   We find ourselves in a rather complicated situation these days, for which reason we are not permitted to speak in public.
2. Pase Ud. a la cocina, _____ las manos, _____ a la mesa y _____ todo lo que allí encuentre.
   Go into the kitchen, wash your hands, sit down at the table, and eat up everything you find there.
3. Una fuerte dosis de ironía _____ en la novela.
   A strong dose of irony shows through (form of **traslucirse**) *in the novel.*
4. Ten los dedos bien juntos para que no _____ ningún granito de arena.
   Keep your fingers close together so that not even a grain of sand gets away from you.
5. ¿ _____ del magnífico gato que te mostré la semana pasada? _____ anoche.
   Do you remember the magnificent cat I showed you last week? He died on me last night.
6. _____ olvidó decirte que _____ en Río de Janeiro hasta recibir nuevas instrucciones mías.
   I forgot to tell you to stay in Rio de Janeiro until you received my new instructions.

7. El enajenamiento que sintió en Nueva York lo obligó a _____ a Wichita lo más pronto posible.
   The alienation he felt in New York forced him to come to Wichita as soon as possible.
8. Será mejor que no _____ con ella ahora, porque está de muy mal humor.
   It will be better for us not to get into it (form of **meterse**) *with her now, because she's in a very bad mood.*
9. Váya_____ Ud. de aquí inmediatamente si no quiere ver_____ con ellos.
   Get out of here right away if you don't want to run into them.
10. _____ fumar en los ascensores.
    Smoking in the elevators is forbidden.

• EXERCISE B

Translate the following sentences to present orally in class.

1. I have planned to go to Montevideo for the winter vacation.
2. The kidnapped man was killed by the guerrillas at the hour indicated.
3. Relax. When the moment arrives, the question indicated is asked of him, the deal agreed on is offered to him, and if he doesn't accept it, he is told where to go (form of **mandar** someone **de paseo**).
4. Spanish spoken. Rags sold wholesale. Rooms for rent.
5. Information is sought concerning the whereabouts of the girl who was seen yesterday in (the) company of the murderer.
6. I got up on the wrong side of the bed (form of **levantarse con las malas**) because I couldn't get to sleep last night until after one o'clock.
7. Once she had told him, she regretted how cutting her words had been.
8. If they don't dare to go alone, we'll all have to get up good and early to accompany them.
9. For heaven's sake, young lady! One doesn't say that in front of such distinguished people.
10. It's becoming obvious that they love each other dearly (**con toda el alma**).

• EXERCISE C

Rewrite each of the following sentences so that the idea involved is expressed in terms of "each other."

   Example:
   Yo miro a Juan y Juan me mira a mí.
   Juan y yo nos miramos.

1. Cándido quiere mucho a Consuelo, y Consuelo lo quiere a él.
2. ¿Ves con frecuencia a tu hermano? ¿Tu hermano te ve a ti?
3. Visito a mis primos todas las semanas, y ellos me visitan a mí.
4. Mario conoció a Susana en Florencia, y Susana lo conoció a él.
5. Marisol no le escribía nunca a su abuelo, y el abuelo no le escribía a ella.
6. Yo le enseñaré a Marcos lo que me regalaron, y Marcos me enseñará lo que le regalaron a él.
7. Tengo entendido que Ud. odia al señor Menéndez y que el señor Menéndez lo odia a Ud.
8. Estoy seguro de que Julián ayudará a Mauricio y que Mauricio ayudará a Julián si surgen problemas.
9. Ramón besó a su novia, y la novia lo besó a él.
10. Yo admiro a mi profesor, y el profesor me admira a mí.

• EXERCISE D

Rewrite the following sentences to eliminate any reference to a particular subject.

Example:
Mi hermanito rompió la ventana.
Se rompió la ventana.

Cristóbal Colón descubrió América en 1492.
América fue descubierta en 1492.

1. Raimundo corregirá las pruebas la semana que viene.
2. La sirvienta ha lavado los platos.
3. Los habitantes de Andorra hablan catalán.
4. Mi hermano construyó una casa el año pasado.
5. Mi tía y mis primas dicen que va a nevar.
6. Las bombas han destruido toda la ciudad.
7. El jardinero plantaba claveles todos los años.
8. Ignacio y yo terminaremos el trabajo mañana.
9. Margaret Mitchell escribió *Lo que el viento se llevó* hace más de cuarenta años.
10. El dictador encarceló a los revolucionarios.

• EXERCISE E

Complete the following sentences as indicated.

1. No sé como _____ Ud. el lujo de salir todas las noches sin _____ por la impresión que causa.
   I don't know how you can permit yourself the luxury of going out every night without worrying about the impression you cause.

2. _____ muy temprano, pero no _____ dormir porque estaba pensando en lo que _____ le había dicho.
   He went to bed very early, but he couldn't get to sleep because he was thinking about what had been said to him.

3. El semestre pasado _____ todos los días. Ahora _____ hace imposible por los horarios que nos tocaron.
   Last semester we used to talk to each other every day. Now it is becoming impossible for us because of the schedules we ended up with.

4. Su conferencia _____ muy bien recibida por todos los concurrentes.
   His lecture was very well received by all those present.

5. Aunque no te sea conocido, haz lo posible por hablarle para que _____ más a gusto.
   Even if he isn't known to you, do everything possible to talk to him so he'll feel more at ease.

6. Los niños _____ al ver entrar a Papá Noel con su bolsa de regalos.
   The children got excited (form of **alborotarse**) *when they saw Santa Claus come in with his bag of presents.*

7. _____ que uno _____ mal después de una experiencia como ésa.
   It's understandable (form of **entenderse**) *that one should feel bad after an experience such as that.*

8. Si no _____ deja de molestarme con lo de los documentos, _____ vuelvo loco.
   If he doesn't stop bothering me with the business of the documents, I'll go crazy.

9. Ese tipo _____ hizo rico de la noche al día. Cuando yo lo conocí no tenía nada.
   That guy got rich overnight. When I met him, he didn't have anything.

10. La universidad _____ cerrada hasta el año que viene por los disturbios políticos.
    The university has been closed until next year because of the political disturbances.

• EXERCISE F

Translate the following sentences.

1. Only courage and perseverance are respected here.

2. The bad thing about the case is that people always change their mind (repent) when it's already too late.
3. He was told not to open his mouth. The fact that it's known all over indicates that he's not to be trusted (form of **no ser de confianza**).
4. When they impose the curfew, it's not permitted for anyone to be on the streets after such and such (**tal o cual**) an hour.
5. Suddenly the lights went out, the door closed, and we found ourselves completely isolated from the group.
6. Shut your mouth, and get to work. How many times do I have to tell you?
7. They did everything possible to convince us that it wasn't good for us, but we didn't pay any attention to them.
8. That was a tremendous mess (**lío**). Everybody was talking to each other at the same time, which caused none of them to understand each other.
9. They were very satisfied with themselves after last night's performance.
10. Why do you get so sad every time I mention that incident to you? Don't you realize it's time now to pass on to something else?
11. Spoken Spanish is sometimes different from what is found in the textbooks.
12. The two old women were insulting each other at the top of their lungs (**a grito pelado**) until the gentleman with the umbrella intervened (form of **interponerse**) and separated them.
13. If you're uncomfortable, take off your shoes and go barefoot. I always feel better that way.
14. Josefina became furious when she found out you had carried off the dinner that she had prepared so carefully.
15. It slipped my mind to tell you that it's not possible for him to attend the meeting today.
16. Drop by here in an hour, and I'll have it ready for you.
17. We stopped because we couldn't stand it any more (form of **no poder más**). We were dead with fatigue, and I almost went to sleep at the wheel.
18. The ring and the earrings were found by the lady with the white hair, but the necklace wasn't found anywhere.
19. It is requested that one not spit on the floor.
20. If the business of Esteban and Graciela is known already, there is no need to beat around the bush (**andar con rodeos**).

• EXERCISE G

Answer the following questions in Spanish.

1. ¿Se ruboriza Ud. al oír un chiste verde?
2. ¿Ha hecho Ud. algo últimamente de que se haya arrepentido?

3. ¿A qué hora suele Ud. levantarse los domingos?
4. ¿Sería Ud. capaz de casarse con alguien a quien no quisiera? ¿En qué circunstancias?
5. ¿Se enojaría mucho su padre si Ud. le faltara al respeto?
6. ¿Se divierte más leyendo una novela o viendo la televisión?
7. Cuando Ud. no está de acuerdo con su mejor amigo, ¿se atreve a decírselo?
8. ¿De qué defectos de los profesores se quejan con más frecuencia los estudiantes?
9. ¿En qué circunstancias se pone Ud. nervioso? ¿Triste? ¿Furioso?
10. ¿Se opone Ud. a que haya pena de muerte en este país?

• EXERCISE H

After carefully reading the selection that follows, identify all reflexive pronouns. Then write a similar paragraph or two in which you make use of those constructions.

Fue una de esas aventuras de chicos de las cuales no puede uno acordarse sin que le brote (brings forth) una sonrisa de añoranza (longing).

Eramos cinco: mis tres hermanos menores, mi mejor amigo Carlitos y yo. Siempre nos pasábamos la mayor parte de la tarde jugando en el patio que se extendía de la casa hasta una pared de ladrillos bien alta que había al fondo. No me acuerdo muy bien, pero Carlitos y yo tendríamos unos diez u once años en aquel entonces. Una tarde en la cual no teníamos nada que hacer, se nos ocurrió ir a visitar a José, otro amigo que se había ido al campo, a la casa de sus padres. Durante la época de las clases José se quedaba con una tía en el pueblo, pero como estábamos de vacaciones, hacía varias semanas que no nos veíamos.

Carlitos tenía dos petizos (ponies). Uno era bien bajito y bastante panzón (fat-bellied). El otro era un poco más grande. Siempre nos divertíamos jugando con ellos en el patio. A veces nos imaginábamos ser vaqueros. Otras veces éramos gauchos. Esta vez nos íbamos de excursión. La casa de José quedaba a unas dos leguas y media del pueblo. Como la distancia era bastante larga, nos pasamos varios días haciendo los preparativos necesarios. Primero tuvimos que asegurarnos de que conocíamos bien el camino para que no nos perdiéramos. Después, cada uno de nosotros se preparó su equipo de viaje: una chaqueta, un sombrero y algo para comer por si nos daba hambre.

Por fin llegó el día tan esperado. A eso de las ocho de la mañana Carlitos se presentó a la puerta del patio con los dos petizos. Nosotros nos habíamos levantado horas antes para terminar los arreglos. Nos habíamos hecho dos sandwiches cada uno, nos preparamos tres cantimploras con jugo de naranja y una con agua. Después de lo que nos pareció una eternidad, nos subimos a los petizos, dos en el más chico y tres en el grande, y salimos rumbo al campo a eso de las diez de la mañana. Al pasar todos nos miraban como a cosa bien extraña, pero no nos preocupábamos por eso porque íbamos tan entusiasmados con el viaje.

El recorrido de dos leguas y tanto, montados como íbamos, no se hace muy rápidamente que digamos. Algo después del mediodía, cuando el sol se dejaba sentir con bastante fuerza, llegamos a la casa de José. Estábamos molidos *(exhausted)*. Nos dolían las piernas, los brazos y partes del cuerpo que no sabíamos que teníamos. José se alegró mucho de vernos, pero su madre se escandalizó bastante por lo atrevidos que habíamos sido. Ella nos hizo acostarnos para descansar un rato y después nos montamos otra vez a caballo y emprendimos el viaje de regreso para llegar antes de que se pusiera el sol.

Se dice que los chicos tienen un ángel que los protege durante sus travesuras. Por lo menos en esa ocasión, se me ocurre que fue verdad.

Nouns
and
Articles

Gender of Nouns

All Spanish nouns belong to one of two groups that are referred to as *masculine* and *feminine*. Since *grammatical* gender is not the same as *natural* gender (sex), this terminology may be somewhat misleading because it can give English speakers who learn about **la mesa**, **la pared**, and **la cárcel** but **el papel**, **el limón**, and **el palacio** an uneasy feeling that Spanish speakers regard tables, walls, and jails as being in some mysterious way female, while papers, lemons, and palaces are male. It might be less misleading to think of the two groups as Class A nouns and Class B nouns or Type I nouns and Type II nouns, although it is true that most nouns referring to female beings are feminine and those referring to male beings masculine. (Note, however, **la persona** and **la víctima**, both of which are always feminine.)

Except for **la mano**, almost all nouns ending in **-o** in modern Spanish are masculine. Nouns like **la moto**, short for **motocicleta**, **la foto**, short for **fotografía**, and **la radio** (which is masculine in some parts of the Spanish-speaking world), short for **radiodifusión**, are apparent exceptions only because they retain the gender of the form from which they are derived.

The majority of nouns ending in **-a** are feminine, but there are more exceptions to this principle than to the preceding one (**-o**   masculine). There is, for example, a fairly numerous group of masculine nouns ending in **-ma**: **el poema, el diagrama, el tema, el aroma**. (These nouns originally came from Greek, where they belonged to the so-called neuter gender.)

Additional feminine nouns include nouns ending in **-dad** or **-tad**, corresponding to English **-ty** (**la universidad, la libertad**); nouns ending in **-tud** (**la virtud, la multitud**); nouns ending in **-umbre** (**la muchedumbre, la servidumbre**); and most nouns ending in **-ión** (**la cuestión, la solución, la religión**).

Some nouns are either masculine or feminine (with no change of ending) depending on the sex of the person referred to. The various **-ista** nouns are the most common example of this: **el** or **la turista, dentista, pianista, izquierdista**.

Plural of Nouns

Nouns ending in an unstressed vowel form the plural by adding **-s** to the singular:
uña, uñas   tribu, tribus

Nouns ending in a consonant or **-y** form the plural by adding **-es** to the singular:
papel, papeles   buey, bueyes

Not many Spanish nouns end in a stressed vowel. Of those that do, some add **-s** in the plural, others **-es**:
sofá, sofás   café, cafés
but rubí, rubíes   bambú, bambúes

Family names usually remain unchanged in the plural:
los González   los Andrade

Nouns ending in an unstressed vowel plus **-s** (primarily **-es** and **-is**) also remain unchanged:
la dosis, las dosis   el jueves, los jueves

The stress normally remains on the same syllable in the plural of a noun as in the singular; this may make it necessary to add or delete a written accent in the plural:
imagen, imágenes   danés, daneses

Note, however, the change in the position of the stress in **régimen, regímenes** (since the stress does not ordinarily move farther into the interior of a word than the third from the last syllable) and **carácter, caracteres**.

Articles

The forms of the definite article (*the*) in Spanish are **el** (masculine singular), **la** or **el** (feminine singular), **los** (masculine plural), **las** (feminine plural), and **lo** (neuter). The forms of the indefinite article (*a* or *an*) are **un** (masculine singular) and **una** (feminine singular). Articles are essentially a specialized kind of adjectives, and the Spanish indefinite article, like any other Spanish adjective, has a plural, **unos** and **unas** (meaning *some*).

The alternate form **el** for the feminine singular definite article is used before stressed **a-** or **ha-**: **el arma**, **el hacha** (but **la armonía**, **la harina**, where the **a-** or **ha-** is not stressed). **Un** instead of **una** before stressed **a-** or **ha-** also occurs, but not quite as consistently: **un arma** or **una arma**.

The neuter definite article **lo** plus an adjective means *that which is (whatever the adjective expresses)*: **lo malo** means *that which is bad*. Often the best English translation of this type of construction is one involving a colorless noun, such as *thing* or *part*: **lo mejor** = *that which is best* = *the best thing about it* or *the best part*.

> Lo interesante es que ellos ni se daban cuenta.
> *The interesting thing about it (the interesting part) is that they weren't even aware of it.*

> Eso fue lo primero que dijo.
> *That was the first thing he said.*

Note also the use of the neuter article **lo** with adjectives and adverbs in sentences like the following.

> No te puedes imaginar lo bonitas que son sus hermanas.
> *You can't imagine how pretty his sisters are.*

> No teníamos ni idea de lo bien que hablaban inglés.
> *We had no idea of how well they spoke English.*

In general, Spanish tends to use the definite article more than English does and the indefinite article less than English does. The following are some common examples of this tendency.

The definite article is used with abstract nouns.

> La paciencia es una virtud que no tienen todos.
> *Patience is a virtue that not everybody has.*

The definite article is used with nouns that make generalizations.

A los gatos les gustan las sardinas.
Cats like sardines.
(Cats in general. Sardines in general.)

El ruso es una lengua interesante.
Russian is an interesting language.
(Russian in general. [But the article is not generally used with
names of languages after the prepositions **de** and **en** and immediately
after a number of common verbs, such as **hablar, entender, saber,
estudiar, enseñar: un profesor de alemán; me escribió en
italiano; no saben japonés.**])

The definite article is used with titles (other than **don** and **doña**), except in
direct address.

El doctor Riquelme no conoce a la señorita Centeno.
Dr. Riquelme doesn't know Miss Centeno.

But: ¿Cómo está usted, profesor Gijón?
How are you, Professor Gijón?

The indefinite article is generally omitted with unmodified predicate nouns that
simply classify people according to features such as their occupation, nationality,
politics, or religion.

Es francesa.
She's a Frenchwoman.

Es periodista.
He's a journalist.

But: Es un periodista muy conocido.
He's a very well-known journalist.
(This statement individualizes him; it doesn't simply place him in a
certain category.)

The indefinite article is often omitted after negative verbs and the preposition
sin, which implies a negative.

No tenía coche.
He didn't have a car.

Salí sin camisa.
I went out without a shirt.

(**No tenía un coche** or **salí sin una camisa** would suggest that he didn't have
even one car or that I went out without even a single shirt.)

Note also the following cases where English uses an indefinite article and Spanish does not.

Cierto estudiante.
A certain student.

Medio kilo.
Half a kilo.

Otro ejemplo.
Another example.

Cien perros.
A hundred dogs.

Mil plátanos.
A thousand bananas.

Tal palabra.
Such a word.

¡Qué fiesta!
What a party!

The definite article (**el**, **la**, **los**, **las**) followed by an adjective, **de** or **que** and with a noun understood but not expressed, becomes a sort of pronoun and expresses the concepts *the . . . one(s)*, *the one(s) belonging to*, and *the one(s) which*: **el abrigo negro y el azul** *(the black coat and the blue one)*, **mis primos y los de Julio** *(my cousins and Julio's)*, **esta película y la que vimos ayer** *(this movie and the one we saw yesterday)*. (See also the remarks on relative pronouns in Chapter 16.)

• EXERCISE A

Use each of the following pairs of expressions in an original sentence, but omit the noun in the second of the two expressions.

Example:
El pañuelo verde y el pañuelo azul.
Me gusta más el pañuelo verde que el azul.

1. el coche de Aurelio y el coche de su hermano
2. la película que vi anoche y la película que vi la semana pasada
3. las rosas amarillas y las rosas blancas

4. los patos domésticos y los patos salvajes
5. la casa de los Echeverría y la casa nuestra
6. el café que nos sirvió mi tía y el café que nos sirvió Raquel
7. el embajador sueco y el embajador irlandés
8. los turistas que hablan español y los turistas que no lo hablan
9. las sobrinas del señor Valenzuela y las sobrinas de la señorita Barrios
10. la profesora guatemalteca y la profesora costarricense

• EXERCISE B

Make each of the following nouns plural, and in addition supply the appropriate form of the definite article.

Example:
Abeja.
Las abejas.

1. chimpancé
2. mapa
3. Ordóñez
4. revolución
5. volumen
6. cualidad
7. dólar
8. reloj
9. sartén *(frying pan)*
10. títere *(puppet)*

• EXERCISE C

Some nouns change their gender according to their meaning. From the list that follows, choose five such nouns and write a pair of sentences for each noun which exemplifies the difference in meaning.

el/la cabeza	el/la cura
el/la capital	el/la coma
el/la guía	el/la frente
el/la corte	el/la policía

• EXERCISE D

Provide the definite or indefinite article only when needed.

1. Su padre es _____ demócrata.
2. Estuvieron aquí todo _____ año pasado.
3. _____ amor es ciego.
4. Carlos Gardel era _____ cantor muy conocido.
5. No pude ir porque no tenía _____ boleto.
6. Es _____ traje muy fino. Me costó _____ mil dólares.
7. Dame _____ otro ejemplo porque no te entiendo.
8. Nunca dije tal _____ cosa en su presencia.
9. Tráigame medio _____ kilo de queso para _____ jueves.
10. Buenas noches, _____ señor González, ¿cómo está _____ señora?
11. No sabes _____ contento que estoy con esta clase.
12. Mi casa y _____ de Juan están muy lejos.
13. _____ portugués es _____ lengua muy bonita.
14. No me gusta _____ comida picante.
15. Están hablando _____ ruso y no entiendo ni papa.
16. No te preparé _____ café porque _____ agua estaba fría.
17. Ya sé _____ difícil que es.
18. Nunca entiende _____ que le digo.
19. Si vieras _____ bonita que está.
20. No toques esa bicicleta. _____ tuya es _____ otra.

• EXERCISE E

Write a sentence with the elements provided. Supply connecting words where needed.

1. profesor / Rodríguez / estar / aquí / mes / pasado.
2. águila / ser / animal / habitar / Andes.
3. ingeniero / Ortiz / ser / persona / dedicada.
4. lavarse / manos / cepillarse / dientes / terminar / comida.
5. secretaria / completar / proyecto / jueves / dos / tarde.
6. necesitar / comprar / otro / paraguas / porque / mío / romperse.
7. fumar / ser / vicio / muy / reprochado / estos / días.
8. por / general / llover / más / primavera / que / verano.
9. madera / ser / menos / pesada / que / plomo.
10. llegar / diez / noche / martes / catorce / agosto.
11. Juan / creer / tener / razón / pero / yo / saber / que / no / ser / verdad.

12. qué / tipo / más / interesante / ser / que / hablar / anoche.
13. curioso / situación / ser / actitud / padre.
14. aprender / lengua / significar / trabajo / devoción.
15. Enrique / ser / alumno / no / ser / profesor / español.
16. irse / sin / abrigo / aunque / cuando / venir / traer.
17. ponerse / pantalones / y / saco / pero / olvidarse / camisa.
18. Jorge / ser / dentista / que / conocer / año / pasado.
19. como / ejemplo / de / que / decirte / leer / esto.
20. tres / cincuenta / docena / ser / precio / extravagante.

• EXERCISE F

Translate the following sentences into Spanish.

1. The difficult part relates to the problem of his birth.
2. Raise your hand only if you are sure of the answer.
3. Freedom is most appreciated when it is lost.
4. The theme of his speech is what interests me most.
5. The sofas which were on sale were really ugly.
6. If you only knew how tired I am.
7. John's stuff has simply disappeared.
8. His father was a lawyer and his mother a professor.
9. A certain friend of yours told me about last night.
10. What a car! If I had a thousand dollars more, I'd buy it.
11. Sugar is another thing I should avoid.
12. The other thing I want you to remember is that she is a very dedicated student.
13. He speaks Spanish, but French causes him many problems.
14. Professor Rodríguez wants to see Miss Santana in his office immediately.
15. It cost three dollars a dozen, and I didn't have even a cent.
16. My books and Maria's are in the dining room.
17. Mr. and Mrs. Morales did not receive the telegram we sent them.
18. I like dogs of any type, but cats drive me crazy.
19. The matter of the money has not been resolved yet.
20. He went without a tie, and they did not let him in.

• EXERCISE G

Answer the following questions.

1. ¿Qué le gusta más hacer los domingos?

2. ¿Tiene Ud. algo interesante que hacer la semana que viene?
3. ¿Qué profesión tiene su padre?
4. De todas las lenguas que Ud. ha oído, ¿cuál le gusta más?
5. ¿Qué encuentra Ud. lo más interesante de esta clase?
   ¿Y lo menos interesante?
6. ¿Sabía Ud. lo fácil/difícil que sería hablar español?
7. Dicen que el amor es ciego. ¿Lo cree Ud.? ¿Por qué?
8. ¿Tiene Ud. un pariente famoso? ¿Quién es?
9. ¿Cuándo es su cumpleaños? ¿Y el día de su santo?
10. ¿A cuánto está el litro de gasolina en estos días?

• EXERCISE H

After reading the following passage, write a one-page composition in which you describe the strangest person you have ever met. Be detailed and precise in your description.

Doña Felisa era una de esas personas que sólo parecen existir en cuentos. Lo triste es que era completamente real. Nunca supimos qué edad tenía, pero sí recuerdo que yo tenía unos siete años cuando la conocí, y que la impresión que me causó fue tremenda.

Le decíamos doña Felisa porque nadie parecía saber su apellido. Algunos le decían "la loca Felisa," pero los adultos siempre nos reprochaban el término por cruel y no apropiado. Para decir la verdad, yo creo que ellos también lo habrían pensado, aunque no lo dijeran delante de los chicos.

Doña Felisa era bajita y muy flaca. Tenía una joroba *(hump)* en la espalda que le daba un aspecto de bruja. El pelo, bastante canoso *(gray-haired)*, lo llevaba siempre atado en una manta sucia de varios colores. La ropa que usaba era increíble. No importaba qué temporada del año, siempre llevaba cinco o seis enaguas *(petticoats)* de todo tamaño, y tres o cuatro vestidos que la cubrían de pies a cabeza. Le gustaba mostrarles a las señoras lo bonitas que eran sus enaguas, especialmente cuando encontraba una de seda. Esa se la ponía por encima de sus vestidos para que todos la vieran. Juntaba todo tipo de cachivaches *(trinkets)* y de animalitos que escondía en los bolsillos y pliegues *(folds)* de la vestidura. Siempre que uno andaba cerca de ella, se oían ruiditos extraños; o maullidos *(mews)* o ladridos, o el pío pío de algún pajarito lastimado que había recogido y metido en alguna parte misteriosa de su indumento *(clothing)*. En los pies llevaba varios pares de medias, siempre de distintos tamaños y colores, y unas zapatillas de lona y suelas de hilo. Al hombro llevaba una bolsa en la cual metía todos los papeles y tarritos *(cans)* que encontraba en la calle. Al terminar de hacer su recorrido, se llevaba su bolsa a la casa, donde amontonaba su contenido por todas partes.

Vivía sola, en un ranchito de barro con techo de paja, en las afueras de la ciudad. Una vez en que no apareció por el barrio durante varios días, algunos de los vecinos fueron al ranchito pensando que tal vez le hubiera pasado algo. La encontraron medio asfixiada, durmiendo debajo de un montón de papeles y trapos *(rags)* sucios que para ella era una cama. Nos dijeron después que casi no pudieron entrar al rancho porque había tanta basura acumulada por todas partes que no cabía ni una persona de pie. Varias de las vecinas se pasaron tres días limpiando la casa y quemando la basura. Le blanquearon la casa por dentro y por fuera. Le pusieron unos mueblecitos que juntaron entre todos. A doña Felisa le dieron un baño y le prepararon una sopa para que recobrara las fuerzas perdidas, pero la pobre quedó tan triste y desanimada por lo que le habían hecho a su casa, que unos días después, la encontraron muerta, envuelta en unos periódicos y abrazando uno de sus perritos.

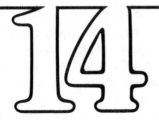

Agreement and Comparison of Adjectives; Adverbs

Agreement of Adjectives

For the most part, only adjectives ending in **-o** in the masculine singular have four separate forms for masculine and feminine singular and masculine and feminine plural: **loco, loca, locos, locas**. Other adjectives have only a singular form (both genders) and a plural form (both genders): **general, generales**. (The plural of adjectives is formed in the same way as the plural of nouns.)

However, the following types of adjectives have separate feminine forms even though they do not end in **-o**.

1. Adjectives of nationality that end in a consonant: alemán, alemana, alemanes, alemanas.

2. Adjectives that end in **-ón** (and the few that end in **-án**): comilón, comilona, comilones, comilonas; haragán, haragana, haraganes, haraganas.

3. Adjectives that end in **-or**, but only those derived from verbs: encantador, encantadora, encantadores, encantadoras (from **encantar**)—but peor, peores; mayor, mayores; inferior, inferiores.

The adjectives **uno, alguno, ninguno, bueno, malo, primero**, and **tercero** (as well as the "literary" adjectives **postrero** and **postrimero**, both meaning *last*) drop the final **-o** before a masculine singular noun: **un buen amigo, el tercer párrafo. Alguno** and **ninguno** acquire a written accent when the **-o** drops: **algún día, ningún problema. Grande** is usually shortened to **gran** before either a masculine or a feminine singular noun: **un gran privilegio, una gran oportunidad. Santo** is shortened to **San** when used as a title before a masculine singular name: **San Francisco, San Ignacio.** (Names beginning with **Do-** or **To-** are exceptions: **Santo Domingo, Santo Tomás, Santo Toribio.**)

Comparison of Adjectives

In traditional grammatical terminology, *good* is referred to as the "positive degree," *better* is the "comparative degree," and *best* is the "superlative degree." To give the sequence *good-better-best* is to "compare" the adjective *good*. With regard to the comparison of adjectives (and adverbs, which are treated the same way), Spanish differs from English in two respects.

First, Spanish has to all intents and purposes lost the distinction between the comparative and the superlative: **más** means both *more* and *most;* **peor** means both *worse* and *worst.* (Spanish does have a so-called absolute superlative, formed with the ending **-ísimo,** which is used to express a very high degree of the concept involved: **interesantísimo** *extremely interesting,* **muchísimo** *a very great deal.*)

Second, English compares some of its adjectives with *more* and *most* (*more ridiculous, most ridiculous*) and others with the endings *-er* and *-est* (*sillier, silliest*), whereas Spanish compares almost all of its adjectives with **más.** The only irregular comparatives are **mejor** *(better, best);* **peor** *(worse, worst);* **mayor** *(greater, greatest, older, oldest);* and **menor** *(lesser, least, younger, youngest).*

Than is usually expressed by **que** in Spanish except before a number, in which case **de** is used.

Julián es más inteligente que Ernesto.
Julián is more intelligent than Ernesto.

But: Ha leído *Don Juan Tenorio* más de veinte veces.
She has read Don Juan Tenorio *more than twenty times.*

When *than,* however, introduces a clause containing a conjugated verb (a verb form that shows person, number, and tense as opposed to an infinitive or a participle), an appropriate form of **del que** is used.

Compramos más libros de los que podemos leer.
We buy more books than we can read.

Están más enfermos de lo que creía.
They are sicker than I thought.

Adverbs

Spanish, like English, uses adverbs to express a wide variety of concepts in areas such as time, manner, place, and degree (**jamás, hoy, así, allá, tan, muy**, etc.). Many of these adverbs, however, are simply vocabulary items and as such do not usually represent any particular problem for English speakers, although the following comments may be worth making.

Sequences like **antes, antes de, antes (de) que** or **después, después de, después (de) que** sometimes confuse English speakers.

Lo había visto antes.
I had seen him before.
(**Antes** is an adverb.)

Hablé con ella antes del desayuno (antes de acostarme).
I talked to her before breakfast (before going to bed).
(**Antes de** is a preposition and is used before a noun [**desayuno**] or a noun equivalent, such as an infinitive [**acostarme**]).

Trataré de terminar el trabajo antes (de) que vuelvan.
I will try to finish the work before they get back.
(**Antes [de] que** is a conjunction and is used to introduce a clause containing a conjugated verb.)

Muy was originally an unstressed variant of **mucho** (the stress fell on whatever followed **muy**) and as such cannot stand alone.

¿Es interesante ese libro? Sí, mucho.
Is that book interesting? Yes, very.

The use of **aquí** and **acá** to mean *here* and of **ahí**, **allí**, and **allá** to mean *there* is a fairly complicated subject, but the following points are worth noting, though they are not hard-and-fast "rules."

Acá is often used with verbs of motion.

Ven acá.
Come here.
(But this does not mean that no one has ever been known to
say **ven aquí.**)

Acá is sometimes more vague and less specific than **aquí.**

En México se toma mucho tequila, pero acá se toma menos.
*In Mexico they drink a lot of tequila, but up here they don't
drink as much.*

The difference between **ahí** and **allí** is theoretically the same as the
difference between **ese** *(that one near you)* and **aquel** *(that one over there):*
ahí is *there near you,* and **allí** is *over there, yonder.* However, many speakers
do not maintain this distinction very rigidly.
   Allá is usually less specific, and sometimes more remote, than **ahí** or **allí.**

Allá en la China no viven como nosotros.
Over there in China (off there in China) they don't live the way we do.

In English, adverbs can be formed from adjectives by means of the ending
-ly (clear, clearly). Similarly, in Spanish adverbs are formed from adjectives by means
of the ending **-mente** (**claro, claramente**). In Spanish, however, this so-called
ending was originally a feminine noun, which accounts for the following facts.
   The ending **-mente** is always added to the feminine singular form of the
adjective (if it has one): **continuamente** from **continuo** (but **generalmente** from
general, which has no distinctive feminine form).
   The ending **-mente** is added to only the last of a series of two or more
adverbs: **lenta y cuidadosamente** *(slowly and carefully).*
   Unlike other Spanish words, adverbs ending in **-mente** can have two strong
stresses in the same word: **cla**-ra-**men**-te, na-tu-**ral**-**men**-te. (However, some
speakers nowadays pronounce these words with only one stressed syllable:
cla-ra-**men**-te, na-tu-ral-**men**-te.)

• EXERCISE A

Change the following phrases into: 1) masculine plural, 2) feminine singular, and
3) feminine plural.

1. un autor famoso
2. el gato negro
3. un alumno inteligente

4. el hombre mexicano
5. mi primo español
6. tu hermano mayor
7. el niño andaluz
8. algún actor francés
9. un amigo mío
10. ningún señor responsable
11. un pato amarillo
12. el ruso simpático
13. un presidente tiránico
14. un bailarín conocido
15. el perro grande

• EXERCISE B

Translate the following sentences to present orally in class.

1. I hope he brings his new car.
2. She always wears that yellow shirt.
3. Each young man should have one.
4. My only hope is that he forgets about it.
5. Studying in Mexico is a great experience.
6. This wine is rather good.
7. The only thing I know is that I am here.
8. Please do all the work before you go out.
9. One other thing, be back at a decent hour.
10. That tall redhead always tells good jokes.

• EXERCISE C

Rewrite the following sentences to express: 1) the "comparative degree,"
2) the "superlative degree," and 3) the "absolute superlative."

Example:
Jorge es inteligente.

1) Jorge es más inteligente.
2) Jorge es el más inteligente.
3) Jorge es inteligentísimo.

1. Este ejercicio es fácil.
2. Mi casa es fea.

3. María Luján era simpática.
4. El examen será difícil.
5. Rosario es amable.

• EXERCISE D

Translate the following sentences.

1. Their house is much bigger than ours.
2. Mary is smarter than Joe.
3. This is the worst book I have ever read.
4. Her best friend promises to come next week.
5. They are poorer than we are.
6. The best part is that you are here again.
7. He is the least capable of all of them.
8. Even the worst thing I could imagine doesn't compare to that!
9. Catalina is tall, Rosa is taller, and Maria is the tallest of all.
10. Each time I see her she gets thinner and thinner.
11. He knows much more than what we had thought.
12. She is more intelligent than he is, but has less confidence in her ability than he does.
13. How many older brothers and sisters do you have?
14. The surprising thing is that the smallest one ran faster and longer than all the rest of them.
15. They are going to need more than $2500 if they are going to buy more than what I showed them last week.

• EXERCISE E

Using the "raw materials" provided in each of the following sentences, make up a new sentence containing a comparison that involves one of the various ways of saying *than* in Spanish.

Example:
Alfonso tiene cinco pesos, pero Ricardo tiene veinte.
Ricardo tiene más dinero que Alfonso.

1. Todos los días compro cinco manzanas, pero me como sólo tres.
2. Milán es una ciudad muy bella, pero no se puede comparar con Roma.
3. Tomás hablaba muy bien el árabe, pero nosotros no lo creíamos.

4. Los cinco libros que están en la mesa son del señor Leal, pero no son todos los que tiene.
5. En comparación con Federico, Ignacio no sabe casi nada.
6. Tú crees que son las cinco, pero en realidad son las siete.
7. Tú no has estado en España tantas veces como yo.
8. Esteban compra muchos libros, pero no puede leerlos todos.
9. No tengo más hermanos que Demetrio.
10. Jerónimo no tiene diez hijas. Tiene menos.

• EXERCISE F

Translate the following sentences.

1. You will have to go quickly if you don't want it to turn out badly.
2. Ironically, he didn't seem very sad when he heard the news.
3. They promised to do it right away, but they work so slowly that I doubt we will have it soon.
4. She spoke timidly at first, but so sweetly that they soon were hanging on every word (form of **estar pendiente de**).
5. I told him frankly and specifically what was troubling me most.
6. By no means will I accept that kind of work. Do it right!
7. They will be here no matter how late it is.
8. Their dog barks loudly and incessantly. I don't know how much longer I can take it.
9. How did you do on your last test? Not too well, but fortunately I passed.
10. Next time do it more carefully. There is simply no reason to continually make the same mistakes.
11. You know as much as I do about that.
12. He reads more rapidly than I do. That's why it's easier for him.
13. If you take one more step backward, you will fall down the stairs.
14. The day before yesterday he seemed to know it all. Now he can't remember a thing.
15. They will discover very quickly what this is all about.

• EXERCISE G

Answer the following questions with a complete sentence.

1. ¿Es Ud. el mejor alumno de la clase? ¿El peor?
2. ¿Habla Ud. mejor el español o el inglés?
3. ¿Tiene Ud. más de diez dólares en el banco?

4. ¿Estudia Ud. más o menos de lo que le sugiere el profesor?
5. ¿Es Ud. mayor o menor que los otros alumnos de la clase?
6. ¿Le costó a Ud. más o menos de ocho dólares este libro?
7. ¿Sabe Ud. más español ahora de lo que sabía al comenzar este curso?
8. ¿Se desayunó Ud. esta mañana antes de venir a clase?
9. ¿Aprendió Ud. el español fácil y rápidamente, o le costó mucho trabajo?
10. ¿Cuál es la idea más sensata *(sensible)* que ha tenido Ud. esta semana? ¿Y la menos sensata?

• EXERCISE H

Write fifteen sentences in Spanish using at least one adverb in each one. Use as many different types of adverbs as you can.

15

Position of Adjectives

A distinction can be made between what are sometimes called *limiting* adjectives and *descriptive* adjectives. Limiting adjectives provide information like which one or how many: our car, that car, the last car, twelve cars. Descriptive adjectives describe: a new car, a small car, a green car, a dilapidated car.

Most of the time limiting adjectives precede the noun in Spanish, just as they do in English, although under certain circumstances they may follow the noun they are used with.

¿Oíste lo que dijo el chiflado ese?
Did you hear what that nut said?
(**Ese** placed after the noun can be somewhat disparaging or uncomplimentary.)

¿Te acuerdas del libro ese que me prestaste el año pasado? Se me ha extraviado.
Remember that book you lent me last year? I've misplaced it.
(Here **el libro ese** has a more vague, indefinite tone than **ese libro**.)

La casa nuestra es mucho más moderna que la de ellos.
Our house is a lot more modern than theirs.

(The possessive follows for emphasis.)

Me apoyaron mis amigos sin excepción alguna.
My friends supported me without a single exception.
(**Alguno,** not normally negative, becomes a very strong negative when
placed after the noun.)

The placing of descriptive adjectives before or after the noun, on the other
hand, is subject to a good deal of variation. Not only is it extremely common for
descriptive adjectives to follow the noun, which they almost never do in English, but
also their placement can be affected by various stylistic considerations (emphasis,
for example, or the general rhythm and balance of a particular sentence) that are not
easy to reduce to "rules." The following points ought to be helpful, but they are
more general principles than hard-and-fast rules.

The commonest reason for including a descriptive adjective is to distinguish or
differentiate the thing it describes from similar things.

En la mesa había un sombrero morado.
On the table there was a purple hat.
(By describing the hat as purple we have differentiated it from other hats
that might have been gray or yellow or blue.)

As the preceding example illustrates, adjectives that have a clearly "differentiating"
function usually follow the noun in Spanish. When there is little or no differentiating
involved, the adjective normally precedes the noun.

El vampiro contempló con deleite la roja sangre de la doncella.
The vampire gazed with delight at the red blood of the damsel.
(Whatever the reason for mentioning that the damsel's blood was red, it
is not to distinguish it from her green blood or her orange blood.)

Quo Vadis es la obra maestra del famoso novelista Sienkiewicz.
Quo Vadis *is the masterpiece of the famous novelist Sienkiewicz.*
(The adjective is not included for the purpose of differentiating the
famous novelist Sienkiewicz from another novelist named Sienkiewicz
who is not so well known, and so it does not follow the noun.)

Adjectives that are to some degree subjective rather than objective (such
as those that express value judgments), or figurative rather than literal, tend to
precede the noun.

La mejor comida del mundo no vale nada sin un buen vino.
The best meal in the world is worthless without a good wine.

Tegucigalpa es una gran ciudad, aunque en realidad no es una ciudad muy grande.
Tegucigalpa is a great city, although it really isn't a very large city.

Pasé la tarde charlando con un viejo amigo.
I spent the afternoon chatting with an old friend (who may not necessarily have been old in the literal sense of elderly*).*

El pobre millonario no sabía qué hacer con su riqueza.
The poor millionaire didn't know what to do with his wealth.

In general, the preceding principles also apply when more than one adjective is used with the same noun: if one adjective is regarded as less objective and "differentiating" than the other(s), it is usually placed before the noun. (In practice, however, there is probably more fluctuation in word order when a noun is modified by two or more adjectives than when it is modified by only one.)

Se casó con una hermosa bailarina española.
He married a beautiful Spanish dancer.

But: Guardó el instrumento en un estuche largo y angosto.
He put the instrument away in a long, narrow case.
(*Long* and *narrow* are regarded as being on about the same level with respect to differentiating force and objectiveness.)

All things being equal, whatever receives the most emphasis or is considered most important in a sentence or any portion of a sentence tends to be put last in Spanish. This general principle underlies, if only indirectly, quite a bit of the placement of adjectives in Spanish, and in some cases it has a very clear and noticeable effect.

La literatura española medieval es más interesante que la moderna.
Medieval Spanish literature is more interesting than modern.
(Emphasis on medieval as opposed to modern.)

La literatura medieval española es más interesante que la alemana.
Medieval Spanish literature is more interesting than German.
(Emphasis on Spanish as opposed to German.)

• EXERCISE A

Some adjectives change their meaning according to the position they have relative to the noun they modify. From the list that follows, choose ten adjectives and write a pair of sentences for each one which reflects the difference in meaning. Translate each sentence into English.

	Before the Noun	After the Noun
antiguo	*former*	*old, ancient*
cierto	*certain, some*	*sure, true*
diferente	*various*	*different*
grande	*great*	*large*
medio	*half*	*average*
mismo	*same*	*very, self*
nuevo	*new (another)*	*brand-new*
pobre	*to be pitied*	*penniless*
propio	*own*	*of oneself*
puro	*nothing but*	*pure*
raro	*infrequent, few*	*odd, strange*
único	*only*	*unique*
viejo	*former*	*old in years*

• EXERCISE B

Translate the following sentences to present orally in class.

1. Modern medicine arose from the witchcraft of past centuries.
2. The Romantic period, although of great importance, was of short duration in Spain.
3. A uniquely beautiful woman like you never passes unnoticed.
4. I can't stand cold coffee. I'd like you to bring me another one that's hotter, please.
5. Buy me a pair of blue pants, two white shirts, a gray coat, and the first pair of black shoes that you find.
6. The white snow covered the whole countryside, wiping out the remains of the bloody battle.
7. My dear friends, I appear before you today to communicate to you the sad news of the demise of a great patriot, an illustrious leader of our revolutionary cause.
8. That lady is driving me crazy with her unbearable and ceaseless talking.
9. In order to protest the racial discrimination that the board of directors (**junta directiva**) of the league is displaying, the best-known players refused to participate in the tournament.
10. The true significance of his actions will not come to be known until after some time.

• EXERCISE C

Complete the following sentences as indicated. Pay close attention to the position of the adjectives.

1. La _____ (only possible explanation) es que el señor no se haya enterado todavía de las _____ (tragic circumstances) que rodean su llegada a este país.
2. Los _____ (tallest boys) se pondrán a la derecha, _____ (those of medium height) al centro, y _____ (the shortest ones) a la izquierda de las _____ (big columns) que allí se encuentran.
3. Las _____ (tall mountains) de la Cordillera de los Andes separan las repúblicas de Chile y la Argentina.
4. En las _____ (leafy branches) de un _____ (gigantic tree) las aves erigen sus nidos con _____ (infinite patience).
5. Una _____ (trembling, feverish hand) acaricia la _____ (fresh, innocent forehead) del niño.
6. El _____ (sad fireplace) no ofrece ya su _____ (morning warmth) a los dos _____ (forgotten little old people) que se acurrucan en un _____ (dark corner) de la casa.
7. Unas _____ (damp, grayish rocks) anuncian la proximidad del _____ (sought-for stream).
8. Un señor de _____ (a dark overcoat), _____ (green beret) y _____ (dark glasses) nos cerró el paso al intentar acercarnos al _____ (student leader).
9. Dentro del _____ (dark room) apenas se divisaba la _____ (vague silhouette) de una _____ (big round table) y dos o tres _____ (broken chairs).
10. Vista _____ (in the faint light of dawn), con su _____ (blonde mane) flotando sobre sus _____ (bare shoulders), más parecía diosa que ser humano.

• EXERCISE D

Translate the following sentences.

1. In the tall grass live a multitude of little animals and wild flowers.
2. The torrential spring rains and the soft winter breezes do not succeed in penetrating the rustic roof that protects us.
3. The two ancient figures strolled through the dirty and narrow streets of the city with slow and tired steps.
4. The strong northerly wind was shaking the heavy wires and filling the horizon with blue sparks.
5. Faded, musty walls enclose the room where the ancient document was found.
6. From the little window located at (in) the top of the tower, a pair of sad, furtive eyes watch the days and years go by.

7. It's impossible to work with her because besides being a capricious and devilish actress, she is demanding too high a price these days.
8. The multicolored stripes that were painted on the horizon announced the end of the hated rains.
9. A famous Spanish writer presented an intimate and inspiring talk on his best known works last night.
10. A vague smile of enchantment appeared on the face of the old woman as she opened again her heavy eyelids.

• EXERCISE E

Answer the following questions.

1. ¿Prefiere Ud. ser una gran persona o una persona grande?
2. ¿Le gusta más llevar ropa formal o informal? ¿Por qué?
3. ¿Hay raros hombres u hombres raros en su clase?
4. Si tuviera Ud. cinco mil dólares, ¿compraría un nuevo coche o un coche nuevo?
5. ¿Quién es y cómo es su mejor amigo?
6. ¿Cuál considera Ud. la lección más fácil de todas las que ha estudiado hasta ahora? ¿Y la más difícil?
7. Describa a la persona que le gustaría ser a Ud. Use por lo menos tres adjetivos.
8. ¿Prefieren Uds. tomar pura agua o agua pura?
9. ¿Cuál le gustaría más, pasar la tarde conversando con un viejo amigo o un amigo viejo?
10. ¿Se considera Ud. medio inteligente o de inteligencia media?

• EXERCISE F

Write a one-page descriptive composition using the beginning and end provided below. Include as many sounds, smells, and visual descriptions as you can. Pay special attention to the position of adjectives.

Era una esplendorosa mañana en las montañas. El sol apenas comenzaba a asomarse por entre los verdes pinos que cubrían las empinadas laderas rojizas. Al plantar el primer pie fuera de la pequeña cabaña donde habíamos pasado la noche, sentimos de un golpe todo el impacto de aquel maravilloso lugar . . .

Regresamos físicamente agotados pero con el espíritu renovado por la hermosura y tranquilidad de esa impresionante naturaleza de la cual nos sentíamos ahora parte.

16

Demonstratives and Possessives

Words meaning *this, that, these,* or *those* are called *demonstratives*. Spanish has three demonstratives. **Este** means *this one here*; strictly speaking, **ese** means *that one there near you,* and **aquel** means *that one over there, that one yonder,* but in a great deal of the Spanish-speaking world, **ese** tends to be used more than **aquel**, and it might not be too great an exaggeration to suggest "when in doubt, use **ese**" as a practical rule of thumb. **Aquel**, however, is certainly perfectly appropriate for referring to something remote in space or time.

Besides the various masculine and feminine forms of the demonstratives (**este, esta, estos, estas; ese, esa, esos, esas; aquel, aquella, aquellos, aquellas**), there are also neuter demonstratives (**esto, eso, aquello**). These neuter demonstratives are used to refer to an idea, a statement, an event, or an unidentified object.

Nadie va a creer eso.
Nobody is going to believe that.

Esto no ocurre con mucha frecuencia.
This doesn't happen very often.

¿Qué es eso?
What is that?

When the masculine and feminine demonstratives are used with a noun, they are called demonstrative adjectives. When the noun is implied but not actually expressed, they are called demonstrative pronouns and are written with an accent to distinguish them from the corresponding adjectives.

El primer artículo me gustó mucho más que éste.
I liked the first article a lot better than this one.

Estas blusas son de Marta, y ésas son de Raquel.
These blouses belong to Marta, and those belong to Raquel.

Unlike the other demonstrative pronouns, the neuters **esto, eso,** and **aquello** do not have written accents since there are no neuter demonstrative adjectives from which to distinguish them.

Este and **aquél** express the concepts *the latter* and *the former* (which in Spanish are mentioned in that order).

Rosette y Eva son buenas amigas, a pesar de que ésta es alemana y aquélla es francesa.
Rosette and Eva are good friends, in spite of the fact that the former is French and the latter is German.

Sometimes the forms of **éste** *(the latter)* are really not much more than ways to say *he* or *she* while making it clear that the reference is to the last person mentioned.

Marisol le pidió dinero a Piedad, pero ésta se negó a dárselo.
Marisol asked Piedad for money, but she refused to give it to her.

The "short" (unstressed) possessives (**mi, tu,** and **su**) are always used in front of a noun. The "long" (stressed) possessives (**mío, tuyo,** and **suyo**) are never used in front of a noun. (**Nuestro** and **vuestro** have no corresponding short forms and are used in both series.) The principal uses of the long forms are the following.

1. After a noun, for emphasis.

La idea tuya es mucho mejor que la de Daniel.
Your idea is a lot better than Daniel's.

2. After a noun, to express the equivalent of English *of* plus a possessive.

Me lo dijo un amigo mío.
A friend of mine told me.

3. Preceded by the appropriate definite article, as a possessive pronoun.

¿Cuáles son los geranios más bonitos, los nuestros o los tuyos?
Which are the prettiest geraniums, ours or yours?
(*The* ones belonging to us or *the* ones belonging to you, hence
the article.)

4. After a form of **ser**, to indicate who owns something.

Dicen que el caballo es suyo.
They say the horse is theirs (belongs to them).

Note the following distinction:

¿De quién es este lápiz? No es mío.
Who does this pencil belong to? It doesn't belong to me.

¿Qué lápiz es éste? No es el mío.
What pencil is this? It's not mine (the one that belongs to me).

In spite of the variety of meanings the forms of **su** and **suyo** can have (*his, hers,
its, yours,* and *theirs*), it is usually clear from the context who they refer to.
However, phrases like **de ella, de ustedes,** or **de ellos** can be used for clarification
if necessary.

El problema de él es mucho más grave que el de ella.
His problem is much more serious than hers.

Spanish generally uses a definite article rather than a possessive in situations,
particularly those involving parts of the body and articles of clothing, in which it is
clear from the context who the possessor is.

Abrí los ojos.
I opened my eyes.

Se quitaron el sombrero.
They took off their hats.

• EXERCISE A

Complete the following sentences as indicated.

1. _____ (this) libro es mío, _____ (that one) es de María, y _____ (that one) es el que le falta a Susana.
2. _____ (this) no puede seguir así. Le dije que aplazaba si no venía, pero ni _____ (that) le importa.
3. Por favor, páseme _____ (that) botella, _____ (this one) está vacía.
4. ¿Qué es _____ (that)? Nunca he visto nada semejante.
5. De todas las casas que vimos, _____ (this one) es la que más me gustó.
6. ¿Ves a _____ (that) señor que está junto a la puerta? _____ (that) es el Sr. Rodríguez.
7. Pepe y Carlota me vuelven loco. _____ (the latter) nunca sabe la respuesta, y _____ (the former) nunca viene a clase.
8. No repitas _____ (that) si sabes que no es cierto.
9. _____ (that) idiota siempre sale con algo _____ (like that).
10. La señora _____ (that woman) de quien te hablé está por cantar.

• EXERCISE B

Translate the following sentences to present orally in class.

1. He always wears that same old shirt and those torn pants.
2. When you finish washing these dishes, put them on the table with those over there.
3. This game is over. Those poor players can hardly walk any more.
4. I want this one, that one, and that one over there.
5. If you really like this one better, take it and leave him that one.
6. I would like this ring, that watch, and those two necklaces that are on the table.
7. That is impossible. This guy always wins.
8. In those days we didn't have to worry about those things.
9. This man is much smarter than that one.
10. I don't think that those problems can be resolved in this manner.

• EXERCISE C

Rewrite each of the following sentences in terms of "the former" and "the latter."

Example:
Rafael habla español y René habla francés.
Este habla francés y aquél habla español.

1. El doctor Febres es psiquiatra, pero el doctor Bravo es cirujano.
2. Mis hermanas trabajan en una fábrica, y mis hermanos en una clínica.
3. Los Dubois son de Francia, y los Schmidt son de Alemania.
4. Las rubias son polacas, y las morenas son griegas.
5. A Manuel le gusta el vino tinto, pero a su primo le gusta más el blanco.

• EXERCISE D

Complete the following sentences as indicated.

1. _____ (my) casa está a una cuadra de aquí, pero _____ (yours) está lejísimo.
2. Esos hermanos _____ (of yours) nunca llegan a hora.
3. Dejé _____ (my) libro, _____ (your) cuaderno, y _____ (her) diccionario en la casa de María.
4. _____ (my) cosas siempre están bien ordenadas, pero vieras las _____ (his).
5. _____ (her) ciudad favorita es París, _____ (mine) Buenos Aires.
6. Ponte _____ (your) abrigo que va a hacer frío.
7. _____ (your) hermano y _____ (my) prima parecen llevarse muy bien.
8. Les dijimos que el coche era _____ (ours), pero no quisieron creernos.
9. ¿De quién es este sombrero? Es _____ (mine).
10. Debes lavarte _____ (your) cara, cepillarte _____ (your) dientes y peinarte. _____ (your) cabello antes de desayunar en _____ (my) casa.

• EXERCISE E

In each of the following sentences replace the second noun by a possessive pronoun.

Example:
La casa de José Luis es más grande que mi casa.
La casa de José Luis es más grande que la mía.

1. Todos dicen que mis geranios son más bonitos que tus geranios.
2. Tu tío habla más idiomas que nuestro tío.
3. Mis hermanas son más bonitas que las hermanas de Alberto.
4. Nuestra madre cose mejor que la madre de esos chicos.
5. Los libros que compró Alejandro son más interesantes que los libros que yo compré.

6. El coche de Andrés costó más que tu coche.
7. Las primas de Mariano bailan mejor que mis primas.
8. Tu toro pesa más que el toro de tus vecinos.
9. Mis alumnas son más aplicadas que tus alumnas.
10. La embajada danesa es más imponente que nuestra embajada.

• EXERCISE F

Translate the following sentences.

1. I like your bicycle much better than mine, but mine is easier to ride.
2. That friend of yours who was here last night must have taken my gloves by mistake.
3. My wish and theirs is that you have a speedy recovery.
4. His pen doesn't write. Would you lend him that one?
5. Our house is much smaller than the one you saw yesterday. That one was theirs.
6. Joe can't come to your party tonight. An aunt of his arrives tomorrow, and he must clean his apartment.
7. Whose purse is this? Oh, that's mine. I have been looking all over the house for it.
8. All my classes are going rather well this semester, but Spanish is my favorite subject.
9. I have three books. One is Maria's, one is John's, and one is mine, but I can't decide which is which.
10. Please put my stuff on the table, his on that chair, and leave yours on the patio until it is dry.

• EXERCISE G

Answer the following questions with a complete sentence.

1. ¿Cuántas personas hay en su familia?
2. Ese libro que Ud. tiene en el escritorio, ¿es suyo o de su compañero?
3. ¿Prefiere Ud. este lápiz que tengo aquí o ése que está en la mesa?
4. Ayer encontré estos tres dólares debajo de esa silla. ¿Sabe Ud. de quién son?
5. Este libro es mío. ¿De quién es aquél?
6. ¿Es suyo ese bolígrafo que tiene Ud. en la mano?
7. Esta silla está rota. ¿Prefiere Ud. sentarse en ésa o aquélla?
8. Mis padres son de Colombia. ¿De dónde son los suyos?

9. Veo que Ud. no trajo su abrigo hoy. ¿Quiere que le preste el mío?
10. Esta pluma mía ya no escribe. ¿Me permite usar la suya?

• EXERCISE H

Read the following paragraph carefully. Then rewrite it, first changing **cámara** to **máquinas**, then to **coche**, and finally to **patines**.

Mira, te pedí que me trajeras la cámara mía, no la tuya ni la de Pepe. La mía es la única que sé usar bien. La tuya es demasiado complicada y la de Pepe pesa mucho. Si hubiera querido la tuya, te la hubiera pedido, pero no la sé manejar. La de Pepe es viejísima, de ésas que usaban en los años cuarenta. Escúchame bien, llévate las de ustedes, y por favor tráeme la que te pedí.

Relative, Interrogative, and Negative Pronouns

Relative Pronouns

The term *relative pronoun* is applied to words like *who* in "the woman who grew these chrysanthemums" or *that* in "the still life that he painted." The relative pronouns in Spanish are **que, quien (quienes), el cual (la cual, los cuales, las cuales,** and the neuter **lo cual),** and **el que (la que, los que, las que,** and the neuter **lo que).** There is also a relative adjective **cuyo (cuya, cuyos, cuyas)** *whose*—**el señor con cuya hija pienso casarme** *the man whose daughter I intend to marry*—but it is not used much in informal conversational style. The English relative pronouns can be omitted under certain circumstances ("the still life that he painted" or "the still life he painted"), but the Spanish relatives cannot.

Que is the commonest relative pronoun in Spanish. It can be used as either a subject or an object, to refer to either people or things.

Me lo dijo un primo mío que es médico.
A cousin of mine who is a doctor told me.

Muéstrame la revista que compraste.
Show me the magazine you bought.

After prepositions, to refer to people, **quien** is used instead of **que**.

Me presentó a una chica con quien trabaja en la oficina.
She introduced me to a girl she works with at the office.

Que is used after prepositions to refer to things, but only after a few very common short prepositions, primarily **a**, **con**, **de**, and **en**. In other cases **el (la) que** or **el (la) cual** is used.

Este es el artículo de que te hablaba.
This is the article I was talking to you about.

But: No abandonemos la noble causa por la cual hemos hecho todos estos sacrificios.
Let us not abandon the noble cause for which we have made all these sacrifices.

Since it can show gender, **el cual** is occasionally useful to avoid ambiguity.

La tía de su marido, la cual es de Ginebra, vive con ellos.
Her husband's aunt, who is from Geneva, lives with them.
("**Que** es de Ginebra" might not make it entirely clear whether it is the aunt or the husband who is from Geneva.)

As simple relative pronouns, **el cual** and **el que** are almost interchangeable; however, only **el que**, not **el cual**, can be used in the sense of *the one who*.

Los que no tienen nada que perder son los obreros.
The ones who (those who) have nothing to lose are the workers.

Similarly, only **lo que**, not **lo cual**, can be used to express non-interrogative *what* (in other words, *that which*).

Me horrorizó lo que me contaron.
What they told me horrified me.

Either **lo cual** or **lo que** can be used as a *neuter* relative pronoun to translate a *which* that refers to a whole clause (a fact, event, statement, idea, etc.).

Dicen que mi padre es letón, lo cual (lo que) no es verdad.
They say my father is Latvian, which isn't true.

Interrogative Pronouns

The interrogative pronouns used in Spanish are **¿qué?**, **¿cuál?**, and **¿quién?** (**¿quiénes?**). Like all other interrogatives in Spanish (such as **¿cómo?** or **¿dónde?**), they have written accents. Note the following points about interrogatives.

Distinguish carefully "**¿Qué es . . . ?**", which asks for an explanation or a definition, and "**¿Cuál es . . . ?**", which asks for a choice.

¿Qué es un gaucho?
What is a gaucho? (What do you mean by the term?)

¿Cuál es la capital de Irán?
What is the capital of Iran? (Which city is it?)

In Latin America both **¿qué?** and **¿cuál?** can be used as interrogative adjectives (as opposed to interrogative pronouns): **¿qué libro?** or **¿cuál libro?** In Spain only **¿qué?** is used as an adjective: **¿qué libro?**

Cuyo *(whose)* is used only as a relative pronoun (**el medico cuya hija vive en Bolivia** *the doctor whose daughter lives in Bolivia*), never as an interrogative. Interrogative *whose?* is expressed by **¿de quién?**

¿De quién es este canguro?
Whose kangaroo is this?

Negative Pronouns

For an English speaker studying Spanish, learning negatives is simply a question of learning vocabulary: **nadie** *(nobody)*, **nada** *(nothing)*, and so on. Only a few points in this area need to be commented on.

If a Spanish sentence is negative, everything in the sentence is negative.

No veo nunca a nadie en ninguna parte.
I never see anyone anywhere.

If a Spanish sentence is negative, some negative must occur earlier in the sentence than the verb. If no other negative precedes the verb, **no** is used with the verb.

> Nunca fumo. No fumo nunca.
> *I never smoke.*

Spanish rarely uses the negative **ninguno** *(no, none)* in the plural.

> No tiene ningún amigo que viva cerca de aquí.
> *He has no friends that live near here.*

• EXERCISE A

Combine each of the following pairs of sentences into a single sentence containing a relative pronoun.

> Example:
> Tienen una tía. Ella vive en Caracas.
> Tienen una tía que vive en Caracas.

1. Busco un libro. Lo estaba leyendo ayer.
2. Tengo dos hijos. Ellos estudian antropología.
3. Conocemos a una señorita. Rafael fue al baile con ella.
4. Dicen que Antonio habla doce idiomas. Eso me parece imposible.
5. Voy a presentarte a un médico. Trabajo con él en la clínica.
6. Hablaron con la prima de Daniel. Ella es de Leningrado.
7. Tenemos un secretario. Sabe hablar alemán.
8. Es un profesor. Estudié con él hace muchos años.
9. Estas son las cartas. Tú me las pediste.
10. En esa ciudad hay una fábrica. Mis primos trabajan en ella.

• EXERCISE B

Complete the following sentences with an appropriate relative pronoun.

1. Mario, _____ estudia medicina, está de vacaciones este mes.
2. _____ me lo traiga primero, recibirá el premio.
3. Me regalaron los dos anillos de _____ te estaba hablando anoche.
4. Esa señora de _____ te hablé ayer acaba de pasar.
5. Mi sobrino, _____ reside ahora en Barcelona, tratará de averiguar su paradero.

6. De todos mis alumnos, esa señorita de azul es _____ más he apreciado este año.
7. Es éste un libro sin _____ no puede usted prepararse para los exámenes.
8. _____ lo sepan, háganme el favor de indicármelo levantando la mano.
9. Este es el volante con _____ se controla la dirección del vehículo.
10. Este señor presume de sabio, _____ parece ridículo, porque lo conozco muy bien.

• EXERCISE C

Translate the following sentences to present orally in class.

1. That novel of Unamuno we were talking about yesterday, what's it called?
2. The thing that bothers me most is that you seem to make an effort not to understand.
3. We spent three weeks in Acapulco, during which we became completely acclimated to the atmosphere.
4. Who are those guys and what do they want?
5. Of all the ones you saw, which did you like best?
6. Everything that has been said is true, but it doesn't convince me.
7. The person I studied with last night did very badly on the test.
8. The president's daughter, who was in Denver last week, will come to Wichita next month.
9. They say that meat is going to go up in price. Buy all you can now in order to save a few dollars.
10. The city we passed through yesterday suffered an earthquake today.
11. The work of that author, who is now in New York, seems terribly interesting to me.
12. Those same students are the ones who a year ago were leading the revolutionary movement. What a change!
13. What is the essential difference between a short story and a novel?
14. What are you?
15. Which of the Quintero brothers are you?

• EXERCISE D

Rewrite each of the following sentences to make it negative.

Example:
Hay algo en la mesa.
No hay nada en la mesa.

1. Siempre les escribo en español.
2. Tengo un amigo que enseña física.
3. Ese autor ha escrito algunas novelas muy buenas.
4. En esta estación del año hay flores en todas partes.
5. Nos contaron algo interesante.
6. Cualquier medicamento es más eficaz que éste.
7. Al mirar por la ventana vi a alguien que pasaba por la calle.
8. Parece que a ese joven le gusta todo.
9. Alfredo les contó unas historias muy divertidas.
10. Van al cine todos los días.

• EXERCISE E

Complete the following sentences with an appropriate relative, interrogative, or negative.

1. De todas esas chicas, ¿ _____ te gusta más?
2. ¿ _____ dijo eso? _____ (none) de los aquí presentes.
3. Yo sé que éste es el mío, pero ¿ _____ es el tuyo?
4. ¿A _____ invitaste a la fiesta de mañana?
5. ¿Con _____ estuviste y _____ es lo que estaban haciendo?
6. ¿ _____ de las dos te gusta más, _____ viste anoche o ésta?
7. Averigua _____ estuvo allí el mes pasado y sabrás _____ lo hizo.
8. Dime con _____ andas y te diré _____ eres.
9. Me preguntó _____ era, pero no se lo supe decir.
10. ¿ _____ alumnos hablan español en la clase?
11. ¿ _____ has estado toda la tarde? Hace tres horas que te esperamos.
12. ¿ _____ le mencionamos eso si sabíamos que se ofendía?
13. ¿ _____ es la casa que vas a comprar?
14. ¿ _____ es el edificio ese que está a la derecha?
15. ¿ _____ son sus características más sobresalientes?

• EXERCISE F

Translate the following sentences.

1. Why don't you want her to bring you anything?
2. I never tell him anything, but he always finds out.
3. She doesn't like not knowing how to do it.
4. They will speak it, but never like you do.

5. The doctor said he is somewhat better, but I don't think he is any better at all.
6. This food tastes better than ever.
7. By tomorrow he won't remember any of the things we told him.
8. Which one of you promised never to return there?
9. What town could this be? I don't recognize a thing.
10. He said he doesn't want anything either, but he is always hanging around.
11. Whose car is that? What car? That one on the corner.
12. I have never known anyone who can dance like you do.
13. More than anything else, he wants to return to his homeland.
14. Never in my life have I been so angry with anyone.
15. Neither Pepe nor Mario has brought anything.

• EXERCISE G

Answer the following questions with a complete sentence.

1. De todas las películas que ha visto Ud. en los últimos dos meses, ¿cuál le gustó más?
2. ¿Hay alguna actividad que le guste a Ud. más que estudiar español?
3. De las clases que Ud. estudia este semestre, ¿cuál es la que le interesa más?
4. ¿De quién es el libro que tiene Ud. en el escritorio?
5. ¿Sabe Ud. algo relativo a lo que ocurre en Centro América en estos días?
6. ¿Qué es lo que más le gusta a Ud. respecto al estudio del español? ¿Y lo que menos le gusta?
7. ¿No conoce Ud. a nadie que tenga un millón de dólares?
8. ¿Le gusta a Ud. el coche que tiene o prefiere comprar otro?
9. ¿Se acuerda Ud. de lo primero que dijo el profesor al entrar a la clase hoy?
10. ¿Conoce Ud. a todas las personas con quienes estudia español?

• EXERCISE H

Refer to Chapter 3, Preterit and Imperfect, Exercise G. Read the short narrative on **figuritas** and prepare twenty questions in Spanish to ask your fellow students. Be sure you use as many different interrogative, relative, and negative pronouns as possible.

Examples:
¿Quién es el que/la que habla?
¿Cómo se conseguían las figuritas?
¿No había ninguna que le faltaba?

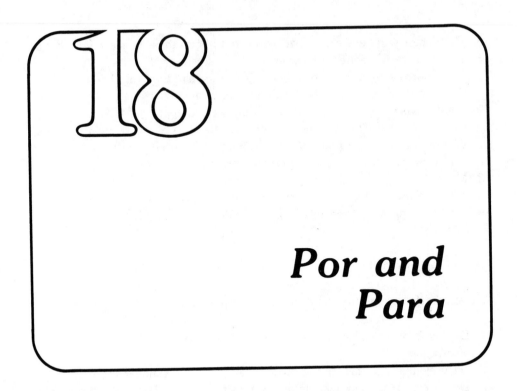

Por and Para

It is difficult to generalize about prepositions, and **por** and **para** are no exception. The following points, however, should provide some guidelines.

Por

In talking about literal physical space relationships, **por** often expresses the route or path followed.

Tendremos que ir por Amberes.
We'll have to go by way of (via) Antwerp.

Ven por aquí.
Come this way.

Andábamos por la Carrera de San Jerónimo.
We were walking along the Carrera de San Jerónimo.

Por can also express a vague, nonspecific location without implying motion along a route or path.

¿Hay un restaurante chino por aquí?
Is there a Chinese restaurant around here?

Me parece que viven por Ventas.
*It seems to me they live somewhere around Ventas
(in the Ventas neighborhood).*

Por can refer not only to space but also to time in a nonspecific way.

Piensan terminarlo por octubre.
*They're planning to finish it around October. (Along in October
sometime. Somewhere around October.)*
(Not as precise as "en octubre.")

Por la tarde suelen ir al cine.
In the afternoon they usually go to the movies.

Por aquel entonces sus abuelos vivían en Cienfuegos.
Around that time his grandparents were living in Cienfuegos.

Por can also express the duration of time.

Vivimos en la selva por treinta anos.
We lived in the jungle for thirty years.

Por is used very extensively to mean *because of* or *on account of*.

Por el calor teníamos que guardarlos en la nevera.
*Because of (on account of) the heat we were having to keep them in
the refrigerator.*

Por no tener adonde ir se quedaba en casa.
*Because he didn't have (on account of not having) anywhere to go he
was staying at home.*

This use of **por** (to express the reason for something, the cause of it) is important not only in its own right but also because it can be used as a kind of general theory of **por** that covers several of its other common uses.

Me dio quinientos dólares por el televisor.
He gave me five hundred dollars for the television set.

(*For* in the sense of *in exchange for* is **por**. The television set was the reason why he gave me five hundred dollars. It was what caused him to give the money to me.)

Está trabajando por su hermano, que está enfermo hoy.
He is working for his brother, who is sick today.
(*For* in the sense of *instead of, in place of,* is **por**. His brother is the reason why he is working; his brother is what is causing him to work.)

Vienen por el dinero a las cinco.
They're coming for the money at five.
(*To come* [or go] *for* in the sense of *to come* [to go] *after, to come* [or go] *to get* is expressed by means of **por**. *The reason why they are coming is to get the money.*)

Estamos dispuestos a hacer cualquier sacrificio por la patria.
We're ready to make any sacrifice for our country.
(*For* in the sense of *for the sake of* is **por**. Our country represents the reason for our making the sacrifice.)

Habla por hablar.
He talks just to be talking.
(He talks for the sake of talking. Talking in itself is the reason why he talks.)

La pirámide fue construida por los egipcios.
The pyramid was built by the Egyptians.
(**Por** expresses the agent by whom something is done. The Egyptians were what caused the pyramid to get built; they were the reason why it got built.)

Somewhat similar to this last usage is the use of **por** to express not only the agent but also the means by which something is done.

Mandamos el paquete por avión.
We sent the package by air (by plane).

Por also expresses the *per* concept.

Una velocidad de 150 kilómetros por hora puede ser peligrosa.
A speed of 150 kilometers per hour can be dangerous.

El ochenta por ciento de los obreros son porteños.
Eighty percent of the workers are from Buenos Aires.

A number of idioms and other set expressions, of which the following are among the most common, involve **por**.

Por ahora (por el momento) no tengo nada que decirte.
For right now (for the moment) I don't have anything to tell you.

El líquido llenaba la botella por completo.
The liquid completely filled the bottle.

Tienen que entregarme sus sugerencias por escrito.
They have to turn their suggestions in to me in writing.

Siéntese, por favor.
Sit down, please.

Por fin cayeron en la cuenta.
They finally caught on.

Por lo general no comemos carne.
As a rule we don't eat meat.

Me lo han dicho por lo menos cinco personas.
At least five people have told me so.

Por lo visto no le importa nada la opinión de los demás.
Apparently the opinion of the others doesn't matter to him at all.

Por poco me caigo al agua.
I almost fell in the water.
(**Por poco** can, as in this example, be used with a verb in the present tense to refer to the past.)

Llévate el impermeable por si acaso.
Take your raincoat just in case.

¿Tienen dinero? Por supuesto.
Do they have money? Of course.

Todos lo tienen por culpable.
Everybody considers him guilty.

Para

Para owes its existence to the fact that at an early stage in the development of the Spanish language it became customary to follow **por** with the preposition **a** in certain situations. (**Para** was originally **pora** in Old Spanish, and **per a**, the Catalan equivalent of **para**, is written as two words even today.) In other words, the final **-a** of **para** was originally **a** meaning *to*, and it may be helpful to remember this since most of the uses of **para** have a sort of *to* quality; that is, they tell where something is going, what its literal or figurative destination is, where it is aimed or headed or directed.

With regard to space relationships, **para** expresses a destination.

> Mañana salimos para Asunción.
> *Tomorrow we're leaving for Asunción.*

> Voy para el banco.
> *I'm heading for the bank. (I'm on my way to the bank.)*

The "destination" of something does not necessarily have to be a literal geographical place.

> Esta carta es para Rogelio.
> *This letter is for Roger.*

The purpose for which something is intended, the goal toward which a thing or an activity is directed, is also a kind of "destination."

> Me dieron veinte dólares para el banquete.
> *They gave me twenty dollars for the banquet. (They gave it to me for the purpose of the banquet, to use toward the expenses of the banquet.)*

> Necesitas estudiar más para la clase de gramática.
> *You need to study more for the grammar class.*

> Contó varios chistes para divertirnos.
> *He told several jokes (in order) to amuse us.*

Para can also express a goal or terminal point in time. It then corresponds to English *by a certain time.*

> Estaremos de vuelta para las siete.
> *We'll be back by seven o'clock.*

> Espero tenerlo terminado para el martes.
> *I expect to have it finished by Tuesday.*

Para corresponds to English *for* when it implies the idea *considering.*

> Es muy grande para su edad.
> *He's very big for his age.*

(He is big considering his age.)

Para ser argentino habla muy bien el inglés.
For an Argentine he speaks English very well.
(He speaks English well considering that he is an Argentine.)

Para is widely used to refer to working for an employer, although there is a good deal of variation in this area in various parts of the Spanish-speaking world.

Mi primo trabaja para la TWA.
My cousin works for TWA.

To be about to is **estar para** in some parts of the Spanish-speaking world, **estar por** in others.

Estaban para salir (por salir).
They were about to leave.

Para is found in a few idioms and set expressions, but not nearly so many as **por**.

Son muy buenos para con sus padres.
They're very good to their parents.

Me duele mucho la garganta, pero la cabeza no me duele para nada.
My throat hurts a lot, but my head doesn't hurt at all.

Se va para siempre.
He's leaving for good.
(But *forever* can also be found expressed by **por siempre**.)

• EXERCISE A

Complete the following sentences as indicated.

1. _____ ahora es suficiente que me entregue el borrador, pero _____ mañana lo necesito terminado.
   For now it's sufficient for you to hand in the rough draft to me, but by tomorrow I need it finished.
2. Como a mí me es imposible dejar el proyecto hoy, mi secretaria dará la presentación _____ mí.
   Since it's impossible for me to leave the project today, my secretary will give the presentation for me.

3. ¿Sabe Ud. _____ casualidad dónde podría encontrar un agente de policía?
Do you know perchance where I could find a policeman?

4. _____ fin te dignaste a regresar; fuiste a Caracas _____ dos semanas y estuvimos mes y medio sin oír palabra.
You finally saw fit to return; you went to Caracas for two weeks, and we didn't hear a word from you for a month and a half.

5. Estuvimos allí _____ dos horas y no conseguimos que nos dieran los documentos _____ entrar al país.
We were there for two hours, and we weren't able to get them to give us the documents for entering the country.

6. Cuando llegues a Denver, pasa _____ mi casa y te entregaré el paquete _____ Eloísa.
When you get to Denver, come by my house and I'll give you the package for Eloísa.

7. ¿Cómo piensa ir a Buenos Aires? ¿ _____ avión, _____ mar, o _____ tierra?
How do you intend to go to Buenos Aires? By plane, by sea, or by land?

8. No se atrevía a decir una palabra _____ temor a demostrar su ignorancia.
He didn't dare to say a word for fear of displaying his ignorance.

9. ¿ _____ cuándo me puedes tener arreglado el reloj que te traje?
By when can you have the watch I brought you fixed?

10. Hombre, ¿estás listo _____ ir o no? El avión está _____ despegar.
Man, are you ready to go or not? The plane is about to take off.

• EXERCISE B

Translate the following sentences to present orally in class.

1. *Mate* is very good for whatever ails you (form of **doler**). At least that's what they say.

2. Generally contributions of less than a dollar aren't accepted.

3. Please don't give him anything for his headache until we know more about his condition.

4. I'm telling you for the fifth and last time. Don't overlook the section on irregular verbs. I'm not the teacher for nothing.

5. For heaven's sake, woman! Don't get involved (form of **meterse**) with those people until you know what their intentions are.

6. For a professor, he knows very little about the subject (**materia**).

7. Send me the order in writing by the last of the month or it won't be possible for me to sell it to you wholesale.

8. They say he was fighting for the good of the country. I believe he was doing it for personal gain (**ganancia personal**).

9. In spite of sharing his concern (**preocupación**) for social injustice, I refuse to accept his position with regard to (**referente a**) education.
10. It was incredible that for a day like yesterday there should be so many people everywhere.

• EXERCISE C

In which of the following sentences would it be acceptable to replace **por** with **para** (or **para** with **por**)? What would the difference in meaning be in each case in which this is possible?

Example:
La casa fue construida por mi hermano.
The house was built by my brother.

La casa fue construida para mi hermano.
The house was built for my brother to own or live in.

1. Es muy inteligente para su edad.
2. Tienes que terminar este trabajo para enero.
3. Ya resolví el problema. Muchas gracias por tu ayuda.
4. ¿Para qué compraste ese libro?
5. A las once fueron por el coche.
6. Su sobrino trabajaba para el presidente.
7. Para no ofenderla, no mencioné el incidente.
8. Me dio diez dólares por la radio.
9. Graciela solía leer cuando menos tres libros por semana.
10. Lo hizo por su abuelo.

• EXERCISE D

Substitute either **por** or **para** for the portion of the following sentences in boldface.

1. Quiero que lo tengas listo **a principios de** abril.
2. Se lo preguntamos a José **a fin de** acabar con esa discusión.
3. Tere y Marucha fueron **a buscar** el auto, pero no han vuelto todavía.
4. Te doy tres figuritas y dos bolitas **a cambio de** tus cuatro mariposas.
5. Pasamos **a través de** esa calle cuando fuimos a la biblioteca.
6. Tuvimos que hacerlo de nuevo **a causa de** todas tus equivocaciones.

7. La secretaria presentó el informe **en lugar de** la directora **a fin de** que la ocasión no fuera una pérdida completa.

8. No sé donde están ahora, pero los vi correr **en dirección a** la cafetería hace unos minutos.

9. **Teniendo en cuenta** lo inteligente que es, me sorprende que haya salido tan mal en esa prueba.

10. **No importa lo** bonito que sea ése, yo prefiero éste.

• EXERCISE E

Complete the following sentences as indicated.

1. Lo encontramos paseándose _____ el jardín, tratando de prepararse _____ la ya impostergable confrontación.
   We found him walking around the garden, trying to prepare himself for the unavoidable confrontation.

2. Me dejaría insultar _____ una de esas señoras sólo _____ ver la cara que pone.
   I would let myself be insulted by one of those ladies just to see the expression on her face.

3. _____ ella no hay nada mejor que un buen libro _____ llenar las horas de ocio.
   For her there's nothing better than a good book to fill her idle hours.

4. Tiene que trabajar hoy _____ la prisa que tuvo al salir ayer.
   He has to work today because of the hurry he was in when he left yesterday.

5. No le mencioné todo lo que sabía _____ no ofenderlo.
   I didn't mention everything I knew to him, for the sake of not offending him.

6. No puedo acompañarte esta noche porque tengo que estudiar _____ el examen de filosofía.
   I can't go with you tonight because I have to study for the philosophy exam.

7. Los pobres dieron la vida _____ devoción a un ideal.
   The poor people gave their lives out of devotion to an ideal.

8. Considerando su actuación esta noche, me pregunto _____ qué equipo juega, ¿el nuestro o el de ellos?
   Considering his performance tonight, I wonder which team he's playing for, ours or theirs?

9. Habla japonés bastante bien _____ lo que ha estudiado.
   He speaks Japanese pretty well for what he's studied.

10. Alcánzame el cachivache ese _____ destapar esta botella.
    Hand me that gadget to uncork this bottle.

• EXERCISE F

Translate the following sentences.

1. Don Ruperto is no longer any good as (do not use **como**) an administrator because he doesn't have the necessary energy.
2. If you want to study to be a dentist, I recommend that you go to Mexico.
3. He promised to send us the money for the ticket, but up to now it hasn't arrived.
4. He gave me four thousand pesos for the book collection I sold him.
5. Let's be walking toward your house while they prepare to receive us.
6. Everything I did, I did for your sake.
7. What I said last night in the speech was mainly for you.
8. I bought him the bicycle for his birthday.
9. They gave me a bottle of wine out of the affection they have for me.
10. Forgive me for bothering you, sir, but I'm calling to postpone the interview we had for today.
11. Last night your brother called about the business of the present for your mother.
12. Write a paragraph about the life of the author, his importance for the present generation, or something of the sort.
13. Why don't you ever go (**pasar**) through Asunción when you're headed for Brazil? Because it's farther for me to go that way.
14. Because you're a student, you have the obligation to prepare yourself every day; at least you have to have read the lesson carefully.
15. Contrary to (**al contrario de**) what is generally believed, those students learn because of and for the teacher they have.

• EXERCISE G

Answer the following questions with a complete sentence.

1. ¿Por qué estudia español? ¿Para qué lo estudia?
2. ¿Cuántos días por semana tiene Ud. clases de español?
3. ¿Para cuándo cree Ud. que hablará español perfectamente?
4. Por lo general, ¿se prepara Ud. para la clase?
5. ¿Para qué ocupación se prepara Ud.?
6. Si Ud. vive en California, ¿por dónde se va a Londres?
7. ¿Cuántas millas por galón le da a Ud. su coche?
8. ¿Cuánto dio Ud. por el libro de español?
9. ¿Por dónde se entra al aula?

10. ¿Es fácil esta lección para Ud.? ¿Y para el resto de la clase?
11. ¿Viene Ud. a la universidad para aprender o sólo por divertirse?
12. ¿Prefiere Ud. viajar por avión, por autobús o por tren?
13. ¿Está Ud. por o en contra del desarmamiento nuclear?
14. ¿Por cuánto tiempo ha estudiado Ud. español?
15. Si yo quisiera comprar su auto, ¿por cuánto me lo vendería Ud.?

• EXERCISE H

Write ten pairs of sentences in Spanish in which **por** and **para** are the only differing elements. Be sure you can explain the difference in meaning for each pair.

Example:
Me dio el dinero para las revistas. (= para comprar)
Me dio el dinero por las revistas. (= a cambio de)

Review Exercises

• CHAPTER 1 **Ser** and **Estar**

Translate the following sentences.

1. It's time for them to be here.
2. Although they now live in Argentina, they are from Italy.
3. Jorge is a good student, but he is tired today.
4. That is a very sad song.
5. I know that Richard is there, and he is so boring.
6. They said it was snowing again in Chicago.
7. Where are you going with that book?
8. The doors were closed by the guard.
9. You look very handsome today.
10. If they are ready, we will begin.

• CHAPTER 2 Stem-changing Verbs

Translate the following sentences.

1. I confess that I don't know how to do it.
2. Close all the windows and doors.
3. We prefer to speak with the boss.
4. They were smiling a minute ago.
5. I don't remember when she said to be home.
6. If Mark doesn't defend us, we are in trouble.
7. She was sleeping when he called.
8. Cross (form of **atravesar**) that street carefully!
9. Please don't laugh when you see them.
10. Our efforts did not yield (form of **rendir**) what we expected.

• CHAPTER 3   Preterit and Imperfect

Translate the following sentences.

1. He was not able to complete the course because his family moved away.
2. I would get up very early, run three miles, shower, and be ready for breakfast by seven o'clock.
3. I'm sorry it bothered you, but I simply had to do it my way.
4. When we left this morning, we didn't realize it was going to be so cold.
5. They wanted to get in to see you, but the guards wouldn't let them.
6. Everything was going perfectly until you showed up.
7. If you didn't want me to tell you, why did you ask me?
8. I spoke to her mother, who said they were going to leave early in order to arrive on time.
9. When we lived there, they always used to stop to visit us.
10. The sign said "Stop," but he ignored it.

• CHAPTERS 4, 5, 6, and 7   The Subjunctive

Translate the following sentences.

1. If I were you, I wouldn't mention that unless she authorizes it.
2. Tell them that they should be here by eight o'clock if they want to go with the group from Montevideo.
3. If it wasn't his, he wouldn't have put it away just like that.
4. Whoever tells me the truth in regard to that will be the one who takes command of the team.
5. Don't worry, provided nobody interferes at the last minute, we're safe.
6. Serve me whatever soup you have ready; I can't wait all day.
7. I don't doubt that you saw him, but, unless he has changed his mind since I talked to him yesterday, you are still in danger.
8. I know that I am the one who told you, but don't repeat it to anybody.
9. If I had known who wrote that work, I wouldn't have had to ask you.
10. She doesn't want you to see her until she has finished putting on her makeup.
11. It's likely that they will get here, but I doubt that they can do it before the train leaves.
12. He asked me to tell you to give it (the watch) to him so he can fix it tonight.
13. If he went to Buenos Aires, he must have seen the Casa Rosada.
14. I need to buy myself a car that uses less gasoline.
15. There isn't anything I prefer to spending these hours with you.
16. Let's tell him the truth, and, if he won't pay any attention to us (**hacernos caso**), he will have to suffer the consequences.

17. If you had been able to get here without them seeing you, just look what a mess (**fíjate el lío**) you would have saved us.
18. They want you to pay them what you owe (**lo debido**) before they find themselves (form of **verse**) forced to take other measures.
19. If you insist on going, at least permit me to accompany you.
20. It's all right for you to talk to him, provided it is with (the) due respect, and not before he gives you the word.
21. What I am hearing is terrible (**tremendo**). I never would have believed it if it weren't you who is asserting it to me (form of **afirmar**).
22. Bring me the dictionary that has those legal terms; these documents are going to drive me crazy.
23. If we lose one more game, the coach will have to look for another job.
24. If it bothers you for me to have to repeat it to you time after time (**vez tras vez**), you'll have to pay more attention.
25. I never would have imagined that you were capable of turning in (**presentar**) such a fouled-up mess (**tal mamarracho**).

• CHAPTER 8   Commands

Translate the following sentences.

1. Don't drink that coffee until it cools.
2. Let's not tell them anything unless they insist.
3. Have John bring it to you tomorrow.
4. Wash those dishes, and dry them before you put them away.
5. Have a good time at the party tonight.
6. Tell me the truth, did you or did you not promise me that you would help them?
7. Sit down, take off your shoes, and rest.
8. Don't ask her to get involved in that business.
9. Let them finish those exercises when they return.
10. Don't get so mad. Wait your turn.

• CHAPTER 9   "Probability" Expressions

Translate the following sentences.

1. She must be mad because she didn't say hello.
2. It was probably the tenth time he explained it.
3. He will probably recite that same old poem again.
4. They must have had trouble, or they would be here.
5. I wonder if she knows you.
6. They probably had done it in a hurry.

7. He wonders if you know what you are saying.
8. It's probably too late to go now.
9. I can't imagine how he could have escaped.
10. Why would they have brought the old car?

• CHAPTER 10 **Hacer** in Time Expressions

Translate the following sentences.

1. We have lived here for four months but still don't know anyone.
2. I saw him only an hour ago.
3. He had been speaking Spanish for two years when we met him.
4. She has known for two weeks that you would be leaving.
5. How many years has it been since you were last there?
6. They said you were to turn it in an hour ago.
7. How long have you been waiting for them?
8. I have not seen her for three months.
9. Pepe had arrived only minutes before.
10. How long had they been living in Rio de Janeiro?

• CHAPTER 11 Personal Pronouns

Translate the following sentences.

1. I saw her and told her what you said.
2. She told John not to bring it to you.
3. They asked Carlos, but he wouldn't tell them.
4. Please take it to her since she can't pick it up.
5. We wanted to buy them for him because he liked them so much.
6. Don't tell me now. I needed to know it yesterday.
7. I have not finished the letter. I was writing it when you called.
8. We brought them for you because it's your birthday.
9. They don't like for you to sell them to her.
10. Mary I spoke to yesterday, but I have not seen Carmen for weeks.

• CHAPTER 12 Reflexives and the Uses of **Se**

Translate the following sentences.

1. She got up, put on her coat, and left.

2. They feel very bad because they could not say good-bye before you left.
3. We were having a good time until he fell down and hurt himself.
4. It is quite obvious that they love each other a lot.
5. One should not say that in public.
6. You can't get in without a ticket.
7. He said that Spanish is spoken in those circles.
8. How does one get to be a lawyer in this state?
9. It is assumed that they will be sorry when they discover the truth.
10. When one studies, this class becomes much easier.

• CHAPTER 13 Nouns and Articles

Translate the following sentences.

1. She speaks German without an accent because she has been there for many years.
2. Forget the part about his past. He is a new man.
3. Dr. Jiménez received the telegram without saying a word.
4. Love is a difficult concept to explain.
5. Put on your coat and tie if you want to make a good impression.
6. Please bring me another one; this map is too old.
7. Let's not mention the business about the test.
8. Those tourists always arrive on Wednesdays.
9. The best part comes right after the battle scene.
10. He likes horses but doesn't have a place to keep (put) them.

• CHAPTER 14 Agreement and Comparison of Adjectives; Adverbs

Translate the following sentences.

1. The third building on the left has to be the one you are looking for.
2. That is the best book I have read in a long time.
3. If he is more intelligent than I, why can't he understand what I tell him?
4. This is much more difficult than he said it would be.
5. Before leaving, he asked me to give you the best seat in the house.
6. Are they happy to be home again? Yes, very.
7. Down there in Argentina they eat a lot of meat.
8. I can hardly hear you. Please speak slowly and clearly.
9. She learns much more quickly than I do.
10. The only thing I can say to you is that he is no longer here.

• CHAPTER 15   Position of Adjectives

Translate the following sentences.

1. That nut always comes out with the same boring story.
2. The big blue car he was driving yesterday belongs to his younger brother.
3. The poor old man could not survive without the help of his good neighbors.
4. That beautiful Spanish guitar was crushed by the heavy truck.
5. Contemporary Latin American literature has influenced many European writers.
6. This cold, humid weather reminds me of the Christmas I spent in Oregon.
7. Put the fresh-cut flowers on the small table near the open window.
8. The small black dog jumped on the dining room table in search of his favorite food.
9. A nuclear war would have unimaginable consequences.
10. That old tape you lent me brings back painful memories.

• CHAPTER 16   Demonstratives and Possessives

Translate the following sentences.

1. I can't believe that this is happening to me.
2. Those two gentlemen standing in the corner want to speak to you.
3. Pepe and Carlos arrived last night. The former is from Costa Rica, and the latter from Brazil.
4. What is this? I ordered fish, not pork.
5. These suitcases are mine, those are hers, and those over there belong to someone else.
6. My things are on the table; please don't mix them with yours.
7. That car of yours runs much better than his.
8. She says this record is hers, but it looks just like mine.
9. Which painting do you like best? His or mine?
10. A good friend of hers told me she had left.

• CHAPTER 17   Relative, Interrogative, and Negative Pronouns

Translate the following sentences.

1. An aunt of his who is a millionaire bought him that car.
2. Show her the present you are going to give them.
3. The man with whom you were speaking is my uncle.

4. The hotel in which we stayed last year is too expensive.
5. Those who have finished may leave now.
6. What he said scandalized the two lawyers sitting at the next table.
7. My mother's brother, who was from Puerto Rico, became a very famous writer.
8. Which of those two do you prefer?
9. He no longer has anything to say to anyone.
10. I don't have any books here that you have not read.

• CHAPTER 18 **Por** and **Para**

Translate the following sentences.

1. You have to go by way of Mexico City to get to Puebla.
2. She was walking through the park when the thief took her purse.
3. Isn't there any place around here where we can eat?
4. Have it ready by Tuesday. That is all I will say for now.
5. If you want to receive credit for those exercises, you will have to present them in writing.
6. Just in case, take five dollars for the ticket.
7. Juan Carlos no longer works for that company. He left for good.
8. We will never know the reason for which he did that.
9. For such a well-known actor, his performance was not that good.
10. If I should not be here by eight o'clock, have Ricardo open the session for me.

Appendix A

Answers To Review Exercises

- CHAPTER 1 **Ser** and **Estar**

1. Es hora de que estén aquí.
2. Aunque ahora viven en la Argentina, son de Italia.
3. Jorge es buen estudiante, pero está cansado hoy.
4. Esa es una canción muy triste.
5. Sé que Ricardo está ahí y él es tan aburrido.
6. Dijeron que estaba nevando otra vez en Chicago.
7. ¿Adónde vas con ese libro?
8. Las puertas fueron cerradas por el guarda.
9. Estás muy guapo hoy.
10. Si están listos, comenzaremos.

- CHAPTER 2 Stem-changing Verbs

1. Confieso que no sé hacerlo.
2. Cierra todas las puertas y ventanas.
3. Preferimos hablar con el jefe.
4. Sonreían hace un momento.
5. No recuerdo cuándo dijo que estuviéramos en casa.
6. Si Marcos no nos defiende, estamos en peligro.
7. Estaba durmiendo cuando él llamó.
8. ¡Atraviesa esa calle con cuidado!
9. Por favor no te rías cuando los veas.
10. Nuestros esfuerzos no rindieron lo que esperábamos.

• CHAPTER 3 Preterit and Imperfect

1. No pudo completar el curso porque su familia se mudó.
2. Me levantaba bien temprano, corría tres millas, me duchaba y estaba listo para el desayuno a las siete.
3. Siento que te molestara, pero sencillamente tenía que hacerlo a mi manera.
4. Cuando salimos esta mañana, no nos dimos cuenta que iba a hacer tanto frío.
5. Querían entrar a verte, pero los guardas no los dejaron.
6. Todo iba pefectamente hasta que apareciste tú.
7. Si no querías que te lo dijera, ¿por qué me lo preguntaste?
8. Hablé con su madre quien me dijo que iban a salir temprano para llegar a tiempo.
9. Cuando vivíamos allí siempre se detenía para visitarnos.
10. El cartel decía "Alto," pero él no le hizo caso.

• CHAPTERS 4, 5, 6, and 7 The Subjunctive

1. Si yo fuera usted, no mencionaría eso hasta que ella lo autorice.
2. Dígales que estén aquí para las ocho si quieren ir con el grupo de Montevideo.
3. Si no era suyo, no se lo hubiera guardado así no más.
4. El que me diga la verdad con respecto a eso, será el que asuma el mando del equipo.
5. No te aflijas, con tal que nadie se interponga a último momento, estamos a salvo.
6. Sírvame la sopa que tenga preparada, no puedo esperar todo el día.
7. No dudo que lo hayas visto, pero a menos que haya cambiado de parecer desde que hablé con él ayer, todavía estás en peligro.
8. Sé que yo soy quien te lo dijo, pero no se lo repitas a nadie.
9. Si hubiera sabido quién escribió esa obra, no te lo hubiera tenido que preguntar.
10. No quiere que la veas hasta que termine de maquillarse.
11. Es probable que lleguen, pero dudo que puedan hacerlo antes que salga el tren.
12. Me pidió que te dijera que se lo des para que pueda arreglarlo esta noche.
13. Si ha ido a Buenos Aires, tiene que haber visto la Casa Rosada.
14. Necesito comprarme un coche que use menos gasolina.
15. No hay nada que prefiera a pasar estas horas contigo.
16. Digámosle la verdad y si no nos hace caso, él tendrá que pagar las consecuencias.
17. Si hubieras podido llegar sin que te vieran, fíjate el lío que nos hubieras ahorrado.
18. Quieren que les pagues lo debido antes que se vean forzados a tomar otras medidas.
19. Si insistes en ir, por lo menos permíteme que te acompañe.
20. Está bien que le hables, con tal que sea con el respeto debido y no antes que él te dé la palabra.

21. Lo que estoy oyendo es tremendo. Nunca lo hubiera creído si no fuera usted quien me lo afirma.
22. Tráeme el diccionario que tiene esos términos legales; estos documentos me van a volver loco.
23. Si perdemos un partido más, el entrenador tendrá que buscar otro puesto.
24. Si te molesta que tenga que repetírtelo vez tras vez, tendrás que prestar más atención.
25. Nunca me hubiera imaginado que usted sería capaz de entregar tal mamarracho.

• CHAPTER 8   Commands

1. No bebas ese café hasta que se enfríe.
2. No les digamos nada a menos que insistan.
3. Que te lo traiga Juan mañana.
4. Lava esos platos y sécalos antes de guardarlos.
5. Que te diviertas en la fiesta esta noche.
6. Dígame la verdad, ¿me prometió o no que les ayudaría?
7. Siéntese, quítese los zapatos y descanse.
8. No le pida que se meta en ese negocio.
9. Que terminen esos ejercicios cuando vuelvan.
10. No te enojes tanto. Espera tu turno.

• CHAPTER 9   "Probability" Expressions

1. Estará enojada porque no saludó.
2. Sería la décima vez que lo explicó.
3. Probablemente recitará esa misma poesía otra vez.
4. Habrán tenido problemas o estarían acá.
5. Me pregunto si te conocerá.
6. Lo habrán hecho a prisa.
7. Se pregunta si sabes lo que estás diciendo.
8. Será muy tarde para ir ya.
9. No me imagino cómo se habrá escapado.
10. ¿Por qué habrán traído el coche viejo?

• CHAPTER 10   **Hacer** in Time Expressions

1. Hace cuatro meses que vivimos aquí, pero todavía no conocemos a nadie.
2. Lo vi hace sólo una hora.

3. Hacía dos años que hablaba español cuando lo conocimos.
4. Hace dos semanas que sabe que te vas a ir.
5. ¿Cuántos años hace que estuviste allí por última vez?
6. Dijeron que tenías que entregarlo hace una hora.
7. ¿Cuánto tiempo hace que los esperas?
8. Hace tres meses que no la veo.
9. Pepe había llegado sólo unos momentos antes.
10. ¿Cuánto tiempo hacía que vivían en Río de Janeiro?

• CHAPTER 11   Personal Pronouns

1. La vi y le dije lo que dijiste.
2. Ella le dijo a Juan que no te lo trajera.
3. Le preguntaron a Carlos, pero él no quiso decírselo.
4. Por favor lléveselo ya que ella no puede pasar a buscarlo.
5. Queríamos comprárselos porque le gustaban tanto.
6. No me lo digas ahora. Necesitaba saberlo ayer.
7. No he terminado la carta. La estaba escribiendo cuando llamaste.
8. Te los trajimos porque es tu cumpleaños.
9. No les gusta que tú se los vendas a ella.
10. A María le hablé ayer, pero a Carmen hace semanas que no la veo.

• CHAPTER 12   Reflexives and the Uses of **Se**

1. Se levantó, se puso el saco y salió.
2. Se sienten muy mal porque no pudieron despedirse antes que te fueras.
3. Nos estábamos divirtiendo hasta que se cayó y se lastimó.
4. Es bastante obvio que se quieren mucho.
5. Eso no se dice en público.
6. No se puede entrar sin boleto.
7. Dijo que se habla español en esos círculos.
8. ¿Cómo se llega a ser abogado en este estado?
9. Se supone que se sentirán mal cuando se sepa la verdad.
10. Cuando uno estudia, esta clase se hace mucho más fácil.

• CHAPTER 13   Nouns and Articles

1. Habla alemán sin acento porque ha estado allá por muchos años.
2. Olvídate lo de su pasado. Es un hombre nuevo.
3. El doctor Jiménez recibió el telegrama sin decir palabra.

4. El amor es un concepto difícil de explicar.
5. Ponte el saco y la corbata si quieres causar una buena impresión.
6. Por favor tráigame otro; este mapa está muy viejo.
7. No le mencionemos lo del examen.
8. Esos turistas siempre llegan los miércoles.
9. Lo mejor viene después de la escena de la batalla.
10. Le gustan los caballos, pero no tiene donde ponerlos.

• CHAPTER 14 Agreement and Comparison of Adjectives; Adverbs

1. El tercer edificio a la izquierda tiene que ser el que buscas.
2. Ese es el mejor libro que he leído en mucho tiempo.
3. Si es más inteligente que yo, ¿por qué no entiende lo que le digo?
4. Esto es mucho más difícil de lo que él dijo que sería.
5. Antes de irse me pidió que te diera el mejor asiento de la casa.
6. ¿Están contentos de estar en casa otra vez? Sí, mucho.
7. Allá en la Argentina se come mucha carne.
8. Apenas te puedo oír. Por favor habla lenta y claramente.
9. Ella aprende mucho más rápidamente que yo.
10. Lo único que te puedo decir es que ya no está aquí.

• CHAPTER 15 Position of Adjectives

1. Ese chiflado siempre sale con el mismo cuento aburrido.
2. El gran coche azul que manejaba ayer es de su hermano menor.
3. El pobre viejo no podría sobrevivir sin la ayuda de sus buenos vecinos.
4. Esa hermosa guitarra española fue aplastada por el pesado camión.
5. La literatura latinoamericana contemporánea ha tenido influencia en muchos autores europeos.
6. Este tiempo frío y húmedo me recuerda la Navidad que pasé en Oregon.
7. Pon las flores recién cortadas en la pequeña mesa que está cerca de la ventana.
8. El pequeño perro negro saltó a la mesa del comedor en busca de su comida favorita.
9. Una guerra nuclear tendría consecuencias inimaginables.
10. Esa cinta vieja que me prestaste me trae recuerdos penosos.

• CHAPTER 16 Demonstratives and Possessives

1. No puedo creer que esto me esté ocurriendo a mí.
2. Esos dos señores parados en la esquina quieren hablar contigo.

3. Pepe y Carlos llegaron anoche. Este es del Brasil, y aquél de Costa Rica.
4. ¿Qué es esto? Yo pedí pescado, no puerco.
5. Estas maletas son mías, ésas son de ella y aquéllas son de algún otro.
6. Las cosas mías están en la mesa; por favor no las mezcles con las tuyas.
7. Ese coche tuyo anda mucho mejor que el de él.
8. Dice que este disco es suyo, pero se parece al mío.
9. ¿Cuál pintura te gusta más? ¿La de él o la mía?
10. Un buen amigo suyo me dijo que se había ido.

• CHAPTER 17   Relative, Interrogative, and Negative Pronouns

1. Una tía suya que es millonaria le compró ese coche.
2. Muéstrale el regalo que les vas a dar a ellos.
3. El hombre con quien hablabas es mi tío.
4. El hotel en el cual nos quedamos el año pasado es muy caro.
5. Los que hayan terminado pueden irse ahora.
6. Lo que dijo escandalizó a los dos abogados sentados a la mesa próxima.
7. El hermano de mi madre, el cual era de Puerto Rico, se hizo un autor muy famoso.
8. ¿Cúal de esos dos prefieres?
9. Ya no tiene nada que decirle a nadie.
10. No tengo ningún libro aquí que no hayas leído.

• CHAPTER 18   **Por** and **Para**

1. Tiene que ir por la ciudad de México para llegar a Puebla.
2. Se paseaba por el parque cuando el ladrón le quitó la bolsa.
3. ¿No hay ningún lugar por aquí donde podamos comer?
4. Téngalo listo para el martes. Eso es lo único que voy a decir por ahora.
5. Si quiere recibir crédito por esos ejercicios, tendrá que presentarlos por escrito.
6. Por si acaso, llévate cinco dólares para el boleto.
7. Juan Carlos ya no trabaja para esa compañía. Se fue para siempre.
8. Nunca sabremos la razón por la cual hizo eso.
9. Para un actor tan bien conocido, su actuación no estuvo tan buena.
10. Si yo no estuviera aquí para las ocho, que Ricardo abra la sesión por mí.

Appendix B

Numbers, Days, Months, Seasons

• Cardinal Numbers

0	cero	**25**	veinticinco (veinte y cinco)
1	uno *(m.)*, una *(f.)*	**26**	veintiséis (veinte y seis)
2	dos	**27**	veintisiete (veinte y siete)
3	tres	**28**	veintiocho (veinte y ocho)
4	cuatro	**29**	veintinueve (veinte y nueve)
5	cinco	**30**	treinta
6	seis	**31**	treinta y uno, -a
7	siete	**40**	cuarenta
8	ocho	**50**	cincuenta
9	nueve	**60**	sesenta
10	diez	**70**	setenta
11	once	**80**	ochenta
12	doce	**90**	noventa
13	trece	**100**	cien
14	catorce	**101**	ciento uno, -a
15	quince	**110**	ciento diez
16	dieciséis (diez y seis)	**200**	doscientos, -as
17	diecisiete (diez y siete)	**300**	trescientos, -as
18	dieciocho (diez y ocho)	**400**	cuatrocientos, -as
19	diecinueve (diez y nueve)	**500**	quinientos, -as
20	veinte	**600**	seiscientos, -as
21	veintiuno, -a (veinte y uno, -a)	**700**	setecientos, -as
22	veintidós (veinte y dos)	**800**	ochocientos, -as
23	veintitrés (veinte y tres)	**900**	novecientos, -as
24	veinticuatro (veinte y cuatro)	**1000**	mil

1100	mil cien	**200.000**	doscientos, (-as) mil
1200	mil doscientos, -as	**1.000.000**	un millón
2000	dos mil	**2.000.000**	dos millones
100.000	cien mil		

Note: Above twenty-nine, the one-word forms are not used.

• Ordinal Numbers

primer(o), -a	first	**sexto, -a**	sixth
segundo, -a	second	**séptimo, -a**	seventh
tercer(o), -a	third	**octavo, -a**	eighth
cuarto, -a	fourth	**noveno, -a**	ninth
quinto, -a	fifth	**décimo, -a**	tenth

• Days of the Week

lunes	Monday	**viernes**	Friday
martes	Tuesday	**sábado**	Saturday
miércoles	Wednesday	**domingo**	Sunday
jueves	Thursday		

• Months of the Year

enero	January	**julio**	July
febrero	February	**agosto**	August
marzo	March	**septiembre**	September
abril	April	**octubre**	October
mayo	May	**noviembre**	November
junio	June	**diciembre**	December

• Seasons

la primavera	spring	**el otoño**	fall
el verano	summer	**el invierno**	winter

Appendix

Personal Pronouns

Subject		Object of Preposition		Reflexive Object of Preposition	
yo	I	mí*	me	mí*	myself
tú	you	ti*	you	ti*	yourself
él	he	él	him		
ella	she	ella	her	sí*	himself, herself
usted (Ud.)	you	usted (Ud.)	you		yourself, itself
nosotros,-as	we	nosotros,-as	us	nosotros,-as	ourselves
vosotros,-as	you	vosotros,-as	you	vosotros,-as	yourselves
ellos	they	ellos	them		
ellas	they (f.)	ellas	them	sí	themselves,
ustedes (Uds.)	you	ustedes (Uds.)	you		yourselves

Direct Object of Verb		Indirect Object of Verb		Reflexive	
me	me	me	to me	me	(to) myself
te	you	te	to you	te	(to) yourself
lo	him, it				
la	her, it	le	to him, to her,	se	(to) himself, herself,
lo, la	you (Ud.)		to you, to it		yourself, itself
nos	us	nos	to us	nos	(to) ourselves
os	you	os	to you	os	(to) yourselves
los	them				
las	them (f.)	les	to them, to you	se	(to) themselves,
los, las	you (Uds.)				yourselves

*After the preposition **con, mí, ti,** and **sí** become **-migo, -tigo, -sigo.**

Verbs

• **A. Regular Verbs**

INFINITIVE

I	II	III
comprar, *to buy*	**vender,** *to sell*	**recibir,** *to receive*

PRESENT PARTICIPLE

comprando, *buying*	vendiendo, *selling*	recibiendo, *receiving*

PAST PARTICIPLE

comprado, *bought*	vendido, *sold*	recibido, *received*

———————————— **SIMPLE TENSES** ————————————

INDICATIVE MOOD

PRESENT

I buy, am buying, etc.	*I sell, am selling, etc.*	*I receive, am receiving, etc.*
compro	vendo	recibo
compras	vendes	recibes
compra	vende	recibe
compramos	vendemos	recibimos
compráis	vendéis	recibís
compran	venden	reciben

IMPERFECT

I was buying, *used to buy, etc.*	*I was selling,* *used to sell, etc.*	*I was receiving,* *used to receive, etc.*
compraba	vendía	recibía
comprabas	vendías	recibías
compraba	vendía	recibía
comprábamos	vendíamos	recibíamos
comprabais	vendíais	recibíais
compraban	vendían	recibían

PRETERIT

I bought, etc.	*I sold, etc.*	*I received, etc.*
compré	vendí	recibí
compraste	vendiste	recibiste
compró	vendió	recibió
compramos	vendimos	recibimos
comprasteis	vendisteis	recibisteis
compraron	vendieron	recibieron

FUTURE

I will buy, etc.	*I will sell, etc.*	*I will receive, etc.*
compraré	venderé	recibiré
comprarás	venderás	recibirás
comprará	venderá	recibirá
compraremos	venderemos	recibiremos
compraréis	venderéis	recibiréis
comprarán	venderán	recibirán

CONDITIONAL

I would buy, etc.	*I would sell, etc.*	*I would receive, etc.*
compraría	vendería	recibiría
comprarías	venderías	recibirías
compraría	vendería	recibiría
compraríamos	venderíamos	recibiríamos
compraríais	venderíais	recibiríais
comprarían	venderían	recibirían

SUBJUNCTIVE MOOD

PRESENT

(that) I (may) buy, etc.	(that) I (may) sell, etc.	(that) I (may) receive, etc.
compre	venda	reciba
compres	vendas	recibas
compre	venda	reciba
compremos	vendamos	recibamos
compréis	vendáis	recibáis
compren	vendan	reciban

IMPERFECT (-ra form)

(that) I (might) buy, etc.	(that) I (might) sell, etc.	(that) I (might) receive, etc.
comprara	vendiera	recibiera
compraras	vendieras	recibieras
comprara	vendiera	recibiera
compráramos	vendiéramos	recibiéramos
comprarais	vendierais	recibierais
compraran	vendieran	recibieran

IMPERFECT (-se form)

comprase	vendiese	recibiese
comprases	vendieses	recibieses
comprase	vendiese	recibiese
comprásemos	vendiésemos	recibiésemos
compraseis	vendieseis	recibieseis
comprasen	vendiesen	recibiesen

COMMANDS

Affirmative—Negative	Affirmative—Negative	Affirmative—Negative
buy	*sell*	*receive*
compra (tú)	vende	recibe
— no compres	— no vendas	— no recibas
compre (Ud.)	venda	reciba
— no compre	— no venda	— no reciba
compremos	vendamos	recibamos
— no compremos	— no vendamos	— no recibamos
comprad (vos.)	vended	recibid
— no compréis	— no vendáis	— no recibáis
compren (Uds.)	vendan	reciban
— no compren	— no vendan	— no reciban

COMPOUND TENSES

The compound tenses of all verbs are formed by adding the past participle to the proper form of the verb **haber**.

PERFECT INFINITIVE

to have bought	*to have sold*	*to have received*
haber comprado	haber vendido	haber recibido

PERFECT PARTICIPLE

having bought	*having sold*	*having received*
habiendo comprado	habiendo vendido	habiendo recibido

INDICATIVE MOOD
PRESENT PERFECT

I have bought, etc.	*I have sold, etc.*	*I have received, etc.*
he comprado	he vendido	he recibido
has comprado	has vendido	has recibido
ha comprado	ha vendido	ha recibido
hemos comprado	hemos vendido	hemos recibido
habéis comprado	habéis vendido	habéis recibido
han comprado	han vendido	han recibido

PAST PERFECT

I had bought, etc.	*I had sold, etc.*	*I had received, etc.*
había comprado	había vendido	había recibido
habías comprado	habías vendido	habías recibido
había comprado	había vendido	había recibido
habíamos comprado	habíamos vendido	habíamos recibido
habíais comprado	habíais vendido	habíais recibido
habían comprado	habían vendido	habían recibido

PRETERIT PERFECT

I had bought, etc.	*I had sold, etc.*	*I had received, etc.*
hube comprado	hube vendido	hube recibido
hubiste comprado	hubiste vendido	hubiste recibido
hubo comprado	hubo vendido	hubo recibido
hubimos comprado	hubimos vendido	hubimos recibido
hubisteis comprado	hubisteis vendido	hubisteis recibido
hubieron comprado	hubieron vendido	hubieron recibido

FUTURE PERFECT

I will have bought, etc.	*I will have sold, etc.*	*I will have received, etc.*
habré comprado	habré vendido	habré recibido
habrás comprado	habrás vendido	habrás recibido
habrá comprado	habrá vendido	habrá recibido
habremos comprado	habremos vendido	habremos recibido
habréis comprado	habréis vendido	habréis recibido
habrán comprado	habrán vendido	habrán recibido

CONDITIONAL PERFECT

I would have bought, etc.	*I would have sold, etc.*	*I would have received, etc.*
habría comprado	habría vendido	habría recibido
habrías comprado	habrías vendido	habrías recibido
habría comprado	habría vendido	habría recibido
habríamos comprado	habríamos vendido	habríamos recibido
habríais comprado	habríais vendido	habríais recibido
habrían comprado	habrían vendido	habrían recibido

SUBJUNCTIVE MOOD

PRESENT PERFECT

(that) I (may) have bought, etc.	*(that) I (may) have sold, etc.*	*(that) I (may) have received, etc.*
haya comprado	haya vendido	haya recibido
hayas comprado	hayas vendido	hayas recibido
haya comprado	haya vendido	haya recibido
hayamos comprado	hayamos vendido	hayamos recibido
hayáis comprado	hayáis vendido	hayáis recibido
hayan comprado	hayan vendido	hayan recibido

PAST PERFECT (-ra form)

(that) I (might) have bought, etc.	*(that) I (might) have sold, etc.*	*(that) I (might) have received, etc.*
hubiera comprado	hubiera vendido	hubiera recibido
hubieras comprado	hubieras vendido	hubieras recibido
hubiera comprado	hubiera vendido	hubiera recibido
hubiéramos comprado	hubiéramos vendido	hubiéramos recibido
hubierais comprado	hubierais vendido	hubierais recibido
hubieran comprado	hubieran vendido	hubieran recibido

PAST PERFECT (-se form)

hubiese comprado	hubiese vendido	hubiese recibido
hubieses comprado	hubieses vendido	hubieses recibido
hubiese comprado	hubiese vendido	hubiese recibido
hubiésemos comprado	hubiésemos vendido	hubiésemos recibido
hubieseis comprado	hubieseis vendido	hubieseis recibido
hubiesen comprado	hubiesen vendido	hubiesen recibido

• B. Stem-changing Verbs

For an explanation of stem-changing verbs, refer to Chapter 2. Some common -ar and -er (e > ie and o > ue) stem-changing verbs are:

acordarse	*to remember*	**empezar**	*to begin*
acostar(se)	*to put (go) to bed*	**encontrar**	*to find, meet*
apretar	*to tighten*	**entender**	*to understand*
ascender	*to rise*	**extender(se)**	*to extend*
atender	*to pay attention*	**jugar**	*to play*
atravesar	*to cross*	**llover**	*to rain*
calentar	*to warm*	**mostrar**	*to show*
cerrar	*to close*	**mover**	*to move*
comenzar	*to begin*	**nevar**	*to snow*
confesar	*to confess*	**pensar**	*to think, plan*
contar	*to count, tell*	**perder**	*to lose*
costar	*to cost*	**probar**	*to test, taste*
defender	*to defend*	**recordar**	*to remember*
descender	*to descend*	**resolver**	*to solve*
desenvolver	*to develop*	**sentarse**	*to sit*
despertar(se)	*to wake (up)*	**soñar**	*to dream*
devolver	*to give back*	**volar**	*to fly*
doler	*to ache*	**volver**	*to return*

Some common -ir (e > ie, i and o > ue, u) stem-changing verbs are:

adquirir	*to acquire*	**morir**	*to die*
arrepentir	*to repent*	**pedir**	*to request*
competir	*to compete*	**preferir**	*to prefer*
conseguir	*to attain*	**referir**	*to refer*
convertir	*to convert*	**reñir**	*to quarrel, scold*
despedir	*to say good-bye*	**repetir**	*to repeat*
divertir	*to amuse*	**seguir**	*to follow*
dormir	*to sleep*	**sentir**	*to feel*
elegir	*to elect, choose*	**servir**	*to serve*
medir	*to measure*	**vestir**	*to dress*

• C. Orthographic-changing Verbs

1. Verbs ending in **-guir** change **gu** to **g** before **a** and **o**.
   seguir   *to follow*
   Pres. Ind.   sigo, sigues, sigue, seguimos, seguís, siguen
   Pres. Subj.   siga, sigas, siga, sigamos, sigáis, sigan

2. Verbs ending in **-gar** change **g** to **gu** before **e**.
   llegar   *to arrive*
   Pret. Ind.   llegué, llegaste, llegó, llegamos, llegasteis, llegaron
   Pres. Subj.   llegue, llegues, llegue, lleguemos, lleguéis, lleguen

3. Verbs ending in **-guar** change **gu** to **gü** before **e**.
   averiguar   *to ascertain, find out*
   Pret. Ind.   averigüe, averiguaste, etc.
   Pres. Subj.   averigüe, averigües, averigüe, averigüemos, averigüéis,
       averigüen

4. Verbs ending in **-ger** and **-gir** change **g** to **j** before **a** and **o**.
   coger   *to catch, seize*
   Pres. Ind.   cojo, coges, coge, cogemos, cogéis, cogen
   Pres. Subj.   coja, cojas, coja, cojamos, cojáis, cojan

   corregir   *to correct*
   Pres. Ind.   corrijo, corriges, etc.
   Pres. Subj.   corrija, corrijas, corrija, corrijamos, corrijáis, corrijan

5. Verbs ending in **-car** change **c** to **qu** before **e**.
   buscar   *to look for*
   Pret. Ind.   busqué, buscaste, etc.
   Pres. Subj.   busque, busques, busque, busquemos, busquéis, busquen

6. Verbs ending in **zar** change **z** to **c** before **e**.
   comenzar   *to begin*
   Pret. Ind.   comencé, comenzaste, etc.
   Pres. Subj.   comience, comiences, comience, comencemos, comencéis,
       comiencen

7. Verbs ending in **-cer** or **-cir** preceded by a vowel change **c** to **zc** before
   a or **o**.
   conocer   *to know*
   Pres. Ind.   conozco, conoces, etc.
   Pres. Subj.   conozca, conozcas, conozca, conozcamos, conozcáis,
       conozcan

8. Verbs ending in **-cer** or **-cir** preceded by a consonant change **c** to **z** before
   a or **o**.
   vencer   *to win*
   Pres. Ind.   venzo, vences, etc.
   Pres. Subj.   venza, venzas, venza, venzamos, venzáis, venzan

9. Some verbs ending in **-iar** or **-uar** take a written accent on the weak vowel when it is stressed.
enviar   *to send*
Pres. Ind.   envío, envías, envía, enviamos, enviáis, envían
Pres. Subj.   envíe, envíes, envíe, enviemos, enviéis, envíen

continuar   *to continue*
Pres. Ind.   continúo, continúas, continúa, continuamos, continuáis, continúan
Pres. Subj.   continúe, continúes, continúe, continuemos, continuéis, continúen

10. In verbs in which an unstressed **i** would fall between two vowels change the **i** to **y**.
leer   *to read*
Pres. Part.   leyendo
Pret. Ind.   leí, leíste, leyó, leímos, leísteis, leyeron
Imperf. Subj.   leyese, etc. *or* leyera, etc.

concluir   *to conclude*
Pres. Ind.   concluyo, concluyes, concluye, concluímos, concluís, concluyen
Pres. Subj.   concluya, etc.
Pret. Ind.   concluí, concluiste, concluyó, concluimos, concluisteis, concluyeron
Imperf. Subj.   concluyese, etc. *or* concluyera, etc.
Imperative   concluye
Pres. Part.   concluyendo

11. Verbs whose stems end in **-ll-** or **-ñ-** lose the **i** of the ending before another vowel.
bullir   *to boil*
Pres. Part.   bullendo
Pret. Ind.   bullí, bulliste, bulló, bullimos, bullisteis, bulleron
Imperf. Subj.   bullese *or* bullera, etc.

reñir   *to quarrel*
Pres. Part.   riñendo
Pret. Ind.   reñí, reñiste, riñó, reñimos, reñisteis, riñeron
Imperf. Subj.   riñese, etc. *or* riñera, etc.

• D. Irregular Verbs

Only tenses which contain irregularities are given.

andar *to walk, go*
Pret. Ind. anduve, anduviste, anduvo, anduvimos, anduvisteis, anduvieron
Imperf. Subj. anduviera, etc. *or* anduviese, etc.

caber *to fit in(to)*
Pres. Ind. quepo, cabes, cabe, cabemos, cabéis, caben
Pres. Subj. quepa, quepas, quepa, quepamos, quepáis, quepan
Future cabré, etc.
Conditional cabría, etc.
Pret. Ind. cupe, cupiste, cupo, cupimos, cupisteis, cupieron
Imperf. Subj. cupiera, etc. *or* cupiese, etc.

caer *to fall*
Pres. Part. cayendo
Past. Part. caído
Pres. Ind. caigo, caes, cae, caemos, caéis, caen
Pres. Subj. caiga, caigas, caiga, caigamos, caigáis, caigan
Pret. Ind. caí, caíste, cayó, caímos, caísteis, cayeron
Imperf. Subj. cayera, etc. *or* cayese, etc.

conducir *to lead, drive*
Pres. Ind. conduzco, conduces, conduce, conducimos, conducís, conducen
Pres. Subj. conduzca, conduzcas, conduzca, conduzcamos, conduzcáis, conduzcan
Pret. Ind. conduje, condujiste, condujo, condujimos, condujisteis, condujeron
Imperf. Subj. condujera, etc. *or* condujese, etc.

dar *to give*
Pres. Ind. doy, das, da, damos, dais, dan
Pres. Subj. dé, des, dé, demos, deis, den
Pret. Ind. di, diste, dio, dimos, disteis, dieron
Imperf. Subj. diera, etc. *or* diese, etc.

decir *to say, tell*
Pres. Part. diciendo
Past Part. dicho
Pres. Ind. digo, dices, dice, decimos, decís, dicen
Imperative di, decid
Pres. Subj. diga, digas, diga, digamos, digáis, digan

Future diré, etc.
Conditional diría, etc.
Pret. Ind. dije, dijiste, dijo, dijimos, dijisteis, dijeron
Imperf. Subj. dijera, etc. *or* dijese, etc.

estar *to be*
Pres. Ind. estoy, estás, está, estamos, estáis, están
Pres. Subj. esté, estés, esté, estemos, estéis, estén
Pret. Ind. estuve, estuviste, estuvo, estuvimos, estuvisteis, estuvieron
Imperf. Subj. estuviera, etc. *or* estuviese, etc.

haber *to have* (auxiliary)
Pres. Ind. he, has, ha, hemos, habéis, han
Pres. Subj. haya, hayas, haya, hayamos, hayáis, hayan
Future habré, etc.
Conditional habría, etc.
Pret. Ind. hube, hubiste, hubo, hubimos, hubisteis, hubieron
Imperf. Subj. hubiera, etc. *or* hubiese, etc.

hacer *to do, make*
Pres. Part. haciendo
Past Part. hecho
Pres. Ind. hago, haces, hace, hacemos, hacéis, hacen
Imperative haz, haced
Pres. Subj. haga, hagas, haga, hagamos, hagáis, hagan
Future haré, etc.
Conditional haría, etc.
Pret. Ind. hice, hiciste, hizo, hicimos, hicisteis, hicieron
Imperf. Subj. hiciera, etc. *or* hiciese, etc.

ir *to go*
Pres. Part. yendo
Past Part. ido
Pres. Ind. voy, vas, va, vamos, vais, van
Imperative ve, id
Pres. Subj. vaya, vayas, vaya, vayamos, vayáis, vayan
Imperf. Ind. iba, ibas, iba, íbamos, ibais, iban
Pret. Ind. fui, fuiste, fue, fuimos, fuisteis, fueron
Imperf. Subj. fuera, etc. *or* fuese, etc.

oír *to hear*
Pres. Part. oyendo
Past Part. oído

Pres. Ind. oigo, oyes, oye, oímos, oís, oyen
Imperative oye, oíd
Pres. Subj. oiga, oigas, oiga, oigamos, oigáis, oigan
Pret. Ind. oí, oíste, oyó, oímos, oísteis, oyeron
Imperf. Subj. oyera, etc. *or* oyese, etc.

poder *to be able*
Pres. Part. pudiendo
Pres. Ind. puedo, puedes, puede, podemos, podéis, pueden
Pres. Subj. pueda, puedas, pueda, podamos, podáis, puedan
Future podré, etc.
Conditional podría, etc.
Pret. Ind. pude, pudiste, pudo, pudimos, pudisteis, pudieron
Imperf. Subj. pudiera, etc. *or* pudiese, etc.

poner *to put, place*
Past Part. puesto
Pres. Ind. pongo, pones, pone, ponemos, ponéis, ponen
Imperative pon, poned
Pres. Subj. ponga, pongas, ponga, pongamos, pongáis, pongan
Future pondré, etc.
Conditional pondría, etc.
Pret. Ind. puse, pusiste, puso, pusimos, pusisteis, pusieron
Imperf. Subj. pusiera, etc. *or* pusiese, etc.

querer *to wish, want*
Pres. Ind. quiero, quieres, quiere, queremos, queréis, quieren
Pres. Subj. quiera, quieras, quiera, queramos, queráis, quieran
Future querré, etc.
Conditional querría, etc.
Pret. Ind. quise, quisiste, quiso, quisimos, quisisteis, quisieron
Imperf. Subj. quisiera, etc. *or* quisiese, etc.

saber *to know*
Pres. Ind. sé, sabes, sabe, sabemos, sabéis, saben
Pres. Subj. sepa, sepas, sepa, sepamos, sepáis, sepan
Future sabré, etc.
Conditional sabría, etc.
Pret. Ind. supe, supiste, supo, supimos, supisteis, supieron
Imperf. Subj. supiera, etc. *or* supiese, etc.

salir *to go out*
Pres. Ind. salgo, sales, sale, salimos, salís, salen
Imperative sal, salid
Pres. Subj. salga, salgas, salga, salgamos, salgáis, salgan
Future saldré, etc.
Conditional saldría, etc.

ser *to be*
Pres. Part. siendo
Past Part. sido
Pres. Ind. soy, eres, es, somos, sois, son
Imperative sé, sed
Pres. Subj. sea, seas, sea, seamos, seáis, sean
Imperf. Ind. era, eras, era, éramos, erais, eran
Pret. Ind. fui, fuiste, fue, fuimos, fuisteis, fueron
Imperf. Subj. fuera, etc. *or* fuese, etc.

tener *to have*
Pres. Ind. tengo, tienes, tiene, tenemos, tenéis, tienen
Imperative ten, tened
Pres. Subj. tenga, tengas, tenga, tengamos, tengáis, tengan
Future tendré, etc.
Conditional tendría, etc.
Pret. Ind. tuve, tuviste, tuvo, tuvimos, tuvisteis, tuvieron
Imperf. Subj. tuviera, etc. *or* tuviese, etc.

traer *to bring*
Pres. Part. trayendo
Past. Part. traído
Pres. Ind. traigo, traes, trae, traemos, traéis, traen
Pres. Subj. traiga, traigas, traiga, traigamos, traigáis, traigan
Pret. Ind. traje, trajiste, trajo, trajimos, trajisteis, trajeron
Imperf. Subj. trajera, etc. *or* trajese, etc.

valer *to be worth*
Pres. Ind. valgo, vales, vale, valemos, valéis, valen
Imperative val(e), valed
Pres. Subj. valga, valgas, valga, valgamos, valgáis, valgan
Future valdré, etc.
Conditional valdría, etc.

venir *to come*
Pres. Part. viniendo
Pres. Ind. vengo, vienes, viene, venimos, venís, vienen
Imperative ven, venid
Pres. Subj. venga, vengas, venga, vengamos, vengáis, vengan
Future vendré, etc.
Conditional vendría, etc.
Pret. Ind. vine, viniste, vino, vinimos, vinisteis, vinieron
Imperf. Subj. viniera, etc. or viniese, etc.

ver *to see*
Pres. Part. viendo
Past Part. visto
Pres. Ind. veo, ves, ve, vemos, veis, ven
Imperative ve, ved
Pres. Subj. vea, veas, vea, veamos, veáis, vean
Imperf. Ind. veía, veías, veía, veíamos, veíais, veían
Pret. Ind. vi, viste, vio, vimos, visteis, vieron
Imperf. Subj. viera, etc. or viese, etc.

Vocabularies

Spanish/English

The gender of nouns (except masculines ending in **-o** and feminines ending in **-a, -ción,** and **-dad**) is indicated by *m.* (masculine) and *f.* (feminine). Most readily identifiable cognates whose meaning is substantially the same in both languages are omitted. Stem-changing verbs are indicated by **ue, ie,** and **i**.

List of Abbreviations

adj.	adjective	*m.*	masculine noun
adv.	adverb	*obj.*	object
conj.	conjunction	*prep.*	preposition
f.	feminine noun	*subj.*	subjunctive
inf.	infinitive	*v.*	verb

• A •

a to
    a pesar de in spite of
    a través de through, across
abeja bee
abrazar to embrace
abrigo coat
abril *(m.)* April
abrir to open
abuela grandmother
abuelo grandfather
aburrirse to be bored
acá here
acabar to finish
    acabar de . . . to have just . . .

acariciar to caress
aceptar to accept
acercarse to approach
aclarar to clear up, explain
acompañar to accompany
aconsejar to advise
acontecimiento event
acordar (ue) to agree
    acordarse (de) to remember
acostar (ue) to put to bed
    acostarse to go to bed
actitud *(f.)* attitude
actividad activity
actuación performance

acuerdo agreement
   estar de acuerdo to agree
acurrucarse to huddle
adelante forward
además also, besides
admirador *(m.)* admirer
admirar to admire
adonde (to) where
adulto adult
advertir (ie) to warn
aeropuerto airport
afligirse to worry, be upset
afueras outskirts
agosto August
agotado exhausted
agradar to please
agradecer to be grateful for
agradecido grateful
agua water
agudo sharp
águila eagle
ahí there
ahora now
ala wing
alcanzar to reach; get up to
   alcanzar a to manage to
alegrarse (de) to be glad
alegre happy
alemán *(m.)* German
alergia allergy
algo something; anything; somewhat
alguien someone; anyone
alguno some; any
alto tall
alumno student, pupil
allí there
amable kind, amiable
amarillo yellow
americano American
amigo friend
amontonar to pile
amor *(m.)* love
anaranjado (color) orange
andaluz Andalusian
andar to go; walk

anillo ring
animado lively, animated
anoche last night
Antártida Antarctic
antemano: de antemano beforehand
anterior previous
antes before
antropología anthropology
anunciar to announce
año year
añoranza nostalgia
apagar to turn off; put out, extinguish
aparecer to appear
apartamento apartment
apellido surname, family name
apenas scarcely
aplazar to postpone; flunk, fail
aplicado studious
apoyar to support; lean
apreciar to appreciate
aprender to learn
apretar (ie) to squeeze
aprobar (ue) to approve; pass (a course)
apropiado appropriate
aprovechar(se) de to take advantage of
apurarse to hurry
aquel that
aquí here
árabe Arabic
arena sand
arreglar to arrange, fix
arreglo arrangement
arrepentirse (ie) to repent
arroz *(m.)* rice
arte *(m. or f.)* art
ascensor *(m.)* elevator
asegurar to insure
asesinar to assassinate, murder
asfixiar to asphyxiate
así thus
asistir (a) to attend
asomarse to appear
aspecto aspect
atar to tie, bind
atención attention; kindness

atrás behind, back
atreverse (a) to dare
atrevido daring
aula classroom
aumentar to increase
aun (aún) still, yet; even
aunque although, even though, even if
ausencia absence
ausente absent
auto car
autobús bus
autor *(m.)* author
autoridad authority
autorizar to authorize
ave *(f.)* bird
aventura adventure
averiguar to ascertain
avión *(m.)* airplane
avisar to notify, let (someone) know
avispa wasp
ayer yesterday
ayuda help
ayudar to help
azúcar *(m.* or *f.)* sugar
azul blue

• B •

bailar to dance
bailarín dancer
baile *(m.)* dance
bajar to go down, come down
bajo low; short
banco bank
bañar to bathe
baño bath
bárbaro barbarous, barbaric
barrio neighborhood
barro mud; clay
basar to base
bastante rather; enough
basura trash, garbage
beca scholarship
besar to kiss

biblioteca library
bicicleta bicycle
bien well; **bien . . .** good and . . . , very
bisabuelo great-grandfather
blanco white
blanquear to whitewash
bobada nonsense
boca mouth
bola ball
boleto ticket
bolígrafo (ball-point) pen
bolsa bag, sack
bolsillo pocket
bomba bomb
bombardeo bombardment
bonito pretty
borde *(m.)* edge
borrador *(m.)* rough draft
botella bottle
brazo arm
brotar to break out, burst forth
bruja witch
bueno good
buscar to look for; go get

• C •

caballo horse
cabaña cabin
cabello hair
caber to fit, have enough room
cabeza *(f.)* head; *(m.)* leader
cachivaches odds and ends, junk
cada each
caer to fall
café *(m.)* coffee
caja box
calentar (ie) to heat
caliente hot
calma calm
calor *(m.)* heat
callarse to be quiet
calle *(f.)* street
cama bed

cámara camera
cambiar to change
cambio change; exchange
    a cambio de in exchange for
camino road
camisa shirt
campo field; country
canción song
candidato candidate
canoso gray-haired
cansado tired
cantar to sing
cantidad quantity, amount
cantimplora canteen
cantor *(m.)* singer
capaz capable
capital *(m.)* capital (money); *(f.)* capital
    (city)
cara face
carne *(f.)* meat
caro expensive, dear
carrera career
carta letter
cartel *(m.)* sign
cartero postman
casa house; home
casado married
casarse to get married
casi almost
caso case
    en todo caso in any case
    hacer caso to pay attention
catorce fourteen
causa cause
    a causa de because of
causar to cause
celoso jealous
cena dinner, supper
centavo cent
centro center; downtown
cepillar to brush
cerca near
cerrar (ie) to close
certeza certainty
cerveza beer

ciego blind
cielo sky; heaven
cierto certain; true
cifra figure, number
cinco five
cincuenta fifty
cine *(m.)* movie theater; the movies
circunstancia circumstance
cirujano surgeon
ciudad city
claro clear; of course
clase *(f.)* class
clavel *(m.)* carnation
cliente *(m. or f.)* client, customer
clínica hospital
club *(m.)* club
cobrar to charge
cocer (ue) to cook
cocina kitchen
cocinero cook
coche *(m.)* car
cola tail; line
    hacer cola to stand in line
colgar (ue) to hang
colombiano Colombian
coma *(f.)* comma; *(m.)* coma
comenzar (ie) to begin
comer to eat
cometer to commit
comida food; dinner
comité *(m.)* committee
como like; as
    ¿cómo? how?
cómoda chest of drawers
cómodo comfortable
compañero companion; friend
comparación comparison
competir (i) to compete
completar to complete
completo complete
complicado complicated
comprar to buy
comprender to understand
comprometido engaged
conceder to grant

concentrar to concentrate
conciencia conscience; consciousness
conciliar to conciliate
    conciliar el sueño to get to sleep
conclusión *(f.)* conclusion
concurrente concurrent; present, in
    attendance
conferencia lecture
confesar (ie) to confess
confiar (en) to trust
conmover (ue) to move
conocer to know; be acquainted with
conocido well-known
conseguir (i) to get, obtain; succeed in,
    manage to
consejero adviser
construir to build; construct
contar (ue) to count; tell
contenido contents
contento happy
contestar to answer
contra against
    en contra de against, opposed to
contrariar to oppose, cross
contratar to contract, hire
contratiempo difficulty
convencer convince
conveniente suitable, desirable, advisable
convenir (ie) to be advisable
conversación conversation
convertir (ie) to convert
    convertirse en to become
cooperar to cooperate
corregir to correct
correr to run
cortar to cut
corte *(f.)* court; *(m.)* cut
cosa thing
coser to sew
costado side
costar (ue) to cost
costarricense Costa Rican
crecer to grow
creer to believe
crimen *(m.)* crimen

crudo raw
cruzar to cross
    cruzarse con to meet, run into
cuaderno notebook
cuadra city block
¿cuál? what? which?
cualidad quality
cualquier(a) any
¿cuándo? when?; **cuando** when
cuanto everything that, all that
    en cuanto as soon as
¿cuánto(s)? how much? how many?
cuarenta forty
cuarto room
cuatro four
cuenta account, bill
    darse cuenta (de) to realize
    tener en cuenta to take into account,
    bear in mind
cuento story
cuerpo body
cuestión *(f.)* question
cuidado care
cuidar to care for
culpa fault, guilt, blame
cultivar to cultivate
cumpleaños birthday
cumplir to fulfill
cuñado brother-in-law
cura *(m.)* priest; *(f.)* cure
curso course

• CH •

champiñón *(m.)* mushroom
chaqueta jacket
charlar to chat
cheque *(m.)* check
chica girl
chico small; boy
chileno Chilean
chimpancé *(m.)* chimpanzee
chino Chinese
chiste *(m.)* joke
    chiste verde off-color joke
chofer *(m.)* driver

• D •

danés Danish
dar to give
dato fact
debajo de under
deber ought, should, must; owe
debido due
decaído feeling bad, low
decidir to decide
decir to say; tell
    no . . . que digamos not . . . to speak of
dedicado dedicated
dedo finger; toe
dejar to leave
    dejar de to cease
delante (de) in front (of)
demás other(s), the rest
demasiado too, too much
demócrata democrat
demora delay
demostrar (ue) to demonstrate
dentífrico dental
dentro inside
deporte *(m.)* sport
derecho right
desanimado discouraged
desaparecer disappear
desarmamiento disarmament
desayunar to have breakfast
desayuno breakfast
descansar to rest
descomponerse to break, get out of order
desconocido unknown
descubrir to discover
desde since
desocupado unoccupied, vacant
despedir (i) to fire; dismiss
    despedirse de to say good-bye to
despegar to take off
despejado (weather) clear
despertar (ie) to wake (someone up)
despertador *(m.)* alarm clock

después after; later
destapar to uncover; uncork
destruir to destroy
desvestir (i) undress
determinar to determine
devolver (ue) to return, give back
día *(m.)* day
    todos los días every day
diablo devil
dibujo drawing
diccionario dictionary
dictador dictator
dicho said, the aforementioned
dieciséis sixteen
diente *(m.)* tooth
diez ten
diferencia difference
difícil difficult
dineral *(m.)* fortune, large sum of money
dinero money
dinosaurio dinosaur
Dios God
diosa goddess
director(a) director
dirigir to direct
    dirigirse to go
    dirigirse a to address
disco record
disgustado unhappy
dispuesto disposed; prepared, willing
distancia distance
distinto different
disturbio disturbance
divertido amusing, entertaining
divertir (ie) to entertain
    divertirse to have a good time
dividir to divide
divisar to perceive, make out
doce twelve
docena dozen
documento document
dólar *(m.)* dollar
doler (ue) to hurt
dolor *(m.)* pain
domesticado tame; domesticated

domingo Sunday
donde where
dormir (ue) to sleep
   dormirse to fall asleep
dos two
dosis *(f.)* dose
duda doubt
dudar to doubt
durante during

• E •

edad age
edificio building
educar to educate
eficaz effective
ejemplar *(m.)* copy
ejemplo example
ejercicio exercise
elección election
elegir (i) to elect; choose
embajada embassy
embajador ambassador
empezar (ie) to begin
empinado steep
emprender to undertake
en in; on; at
enagua petticoat
enajenamiento alienation
enamorado in love
enamorarse (de) to fall in love (with)
encarcelar to imprison
encargar to order (goods, etc.)
encima above, on top
   quitarse de encima to get rid of
encontrar (ue) to find
enero January
enfermarse to get sick
enfermedad disease, illness
enfermo sick
enojado angry
enojarse to get mad
enredo mix-up
Enrique Henry

enseñar to teach; show
ensuciarse to get dirty
entender (ie) understand
enterarse (de) to find out
entonces then
   en aquel entonces at that time
entrada entrance; ticket
entrar to enter, go in, come in
entre between; among
entregar to deliver, turn over, hand in
entusiasmado enthusiastic
envuelto wrapped
época period
equipo team; equipment
equivocado mistaken; wrong
equivocarse to make a mistake, be
   mistaken
erigir to erect
esconder to hide
escribir to write
   escribir a máquina to type
escrito written
   por escrito in writing
escritorio desk
escuchar to listen (to)
escuela school
ese that
   a eso de at about
esforzarse (ue) to make an effort
espalda back
español *(m.)* Spanish
esparcir to scatter, spread
especie *(f.)* sort, kind
espera waiting
   en espera de waiting for, expecting
esperar to hope; wait (for); expect
espíritu *(m.)* spirit
esplendoroso splendid
establecer to establish
estación station; season
Estados Unidos United States
estar to be
este this
estimado esteemed, dear
estudiar to study

estudio study
estúpido stupid
eternidad eternity
evidente evident, obvious
examen *(m.)* exam
exigir to demand
existir to exist
explicar to explain
expresar to express
extranjero foreign
extraño strange
extravagante odd; extravagant

• F •

fábrica factory
fácil easy
facilitar to facilitate, let (someone) have (something)
falta lack; need
    hacer falta to be lacking, be needed
    sin falta without fail
faltar to be lacking, be missing
falla fault, defect
familia family
famoso famous
fantástico fantastic
fastidioso unpleasant
favorito favorite
feliz happy
feo ugly
fiebre *(f.)* fever
fiesta party
filosofía philosophy
fin end
    a fin de in order to
    a fin de que in order that
    al fin y al cabo after all
    fin de semana weekend
    por fin at last
finalizar to finish, conclude
fino fine
física physics
físico physical

flaco thin
flecha arrow
flor *(f.)* flower
Florencia Florence
flotar to float
fondo bottom; back(ground); far end
fortuna fortune
foto *(f.)* picture, photograph
francés *(m.)* French
Francia France
franco frank
franqueza frankness
frecuencia frequency
freír (i) to fry
frente *(m.)* front; *(f.)* forehead
frío cold
fruta fruit
fuente *(f.)* fountain
fuera outside
fuerte strong
fuerza strength, force
fumar to smoke
funcionar to function; to run, work (machines)
furioso furious
fútbol *(m.)* soccer

• G •

Galia Gaul
galón *(m.)* gallon
gana desire
    tener ganas de to feel like, want to
ganar to win; earn; beat (someone at something)
gasolina gasoline
gastar to spend
gasto expense
gato cat
general general
    por lo general in general, as a rule
geranio geranium
gerente manager
gobierno government

golpe *(m.)* blow
    de un golpe all of a sudden
gorila *(m.)* gorilla
gramática grammar
grande large, big; great
grano grain
    llegar al grano to get to the point
griego Greek
grillo cricket
Groenlandia Greenland
grupo group
guante *(m.)* glove
guatemalteco Guatemalan
guerra war
guía *(m.)* guide; *(f.)* guidebook, directory
guitarra guitar
gustar to be pleasing
gusto pleasure
    a gusto at ease, comfortable

• H •

haber there to be
habitante *(m.)* inhabitant
habitar to inhabit
hablar *n. (m.)* speech; *v.* to speak
    de habla española Spanish-speaking
hacer to do; make
hambre *(f.)* hunger
    pasar hambre to go hungry
hasta until
helado ice cream
heredar to inherit
hermano brother
hermoso beautiful
hermosura beauty
hija daughter
hijo son
hilo thread, string
himenópteros hymenoptera
historia history; story
hola hello, hi
hombre man
hombro shoulder

hora hour; time
horario schedule
hoy today
huevo egg

• I •

idea idea
idioma *(m.)* language
igual equal, the same
ileso uninjured, unharmed
imaginar to imagine
impacientarse to get impatient
impedir (i) to prevent
imponente imposing
imponer to impose
importante important
importar to matter
imposible impossible
impostergable unavoidable
impresionante impressive
impuesto tax
incapacidad incapacity
incesante ceaseless
incidente *(m.)* incident
increíble incredible
incurrir to incur
indicación indication
indicar to indicate; tell
indispensable indispensable
indumento clothing
informe *(m.)* report
ingeniero engineer
inglés *(m.)* English
inmediatamente immediately
inmenso immense
insistir (en) to insist (on)
insomnio insomnia
insoportable unbearable
insurgente insurgent
inteligente intelligent
intentar to attempt
interesante interesting
interesar to interest

intervención intervention
íntimo intimate
inventar to invent
invitar to invite
ir to go
    irse to go away
irlandés *(m.)* Irish
ironía irony
izquierdo left

• J •

jabón *(m.)* soap
Japón Japan
japonés *(m.)* Japanese
jardín *(m.)* garden
jardinero gardener
jefatura headquarters
jefe *(m.)* boss
jirafa giraffe
Jorge George
joroba hump
Juan John
juego game
jueves *(m.)* Thursday
jugar (ue) to play
jugo juice
junta board, council
    junta directiva governing board,
    board of directors
juntar to gather, collect
junto a next to, by
juntos together
justo just, fair

• L •

ladera slope
ladrar to bark
ladrido barking
ladrillo brick
lamentable lamentable, deplorable
lápiz *(m.)* pencil

largo long
lastimar to hurt
lavar to wash
lección lesson
leche *(f.)* milk
leer to read
legua league (about 3 miles)
legumbre *(f.)* vegetable
lejos far
lengua language; tongue
    lengua materna mother tongue
Leningrado Leningrad
lepra leprosy
letra letter (of the alphabet)
levantar to lift, raise
    levantarse to get up
libertad liberty
libro book
licenciado lawyer
limpiar to clean
lindo pretty
listo ready; smart
litro liter
loco crazy
lograr to succeed in, achieve
lona canvas
Londres London
luego then
    luego que as soon as
lugar *(m.)* place
Luisiana Louisiana
lujo luxury
luz *(f.)* light

• LL •

llamada call
llamar to call; knock
llave *(f.)* key
llegada arrival
llegar to arrive
llenar to fill
llevar to carry; take; wear
    llevarse to take away, carry off

llevarse bien to get along well
   llevar a cabo to bring off
llorar to cry
llover (ue) to rain

• M •

madera wood
magia magic
mal bad, badly
malabarista *(m. or f.)* juggler
mamá mother
mandar to send; order, command
manejar to manage, handle; drive
manera way, manner
manicomio insane asylum
mano *(f.)* hand
manta blanket; shawl
manzana apple
mañana tomorrow; morning
   pasado mañana the day after
   tomorrow
mapa *(m.)* map
máquina machine
mar *(m.)* sea
maravilla marvel, wonder
maravilloso marvelous, wonderful
mariposa butterfly
Marte Mars
martes Tuesday
más more
matemáticas mathematics
maullido miaowing
mayo May
mayor older, oldest; greater, greatest
mayoría majority
máximo maximum, greatest
médico doctor
media stocking
medicamento medicine
medio means
medio half
mediodía *(m.)* noon
medir (i) to measure
mejor better, best

mejorar to improve
memoria memory
   de memoria by heart
mencionar to mention
menor younger, youngest; smallest, least
menos less
   a menos que unless
   cuando menos at least
   por lo menos at least
mentir (ie) to lie
mentira lie
mes *(m.)* month
mesa table
meter to put
   meterse en to get into, get
   involved in
metro meter
miedo fear
   tener miedo to be afraid
mientras while
mil thousand
milagro miracle
milla mile
millón million
millonario millionaire
minuto minute
mirada look, glance
mirar to look at, watch
mismo same; (one)self
modo way, manner
mojar to wet
mole poblano type of sauce
molestar to bother
molido worn out
momento moment
montado mounted, riding
montar to mount
montón *(m.)* pile
morder (ue) to bite
moreno brunet, dark
morir (ue) to die
mostrar (ue) to show
motivo motive, reason
muchacha girl
mucho much

mueble *(m.)* piece of furniture
muerte *(f.)* death
muerto dead
mundial *(adj.)* world
mundo world
muy much

• N •

nacer to be born
nacionalidad nationality
nada nothing
nadie no one
naranja orange
naturaleza nature
Navidad Christmas
necesario necessary
necesidad necessity, need
necesitar to need
negar (ie) to deny
    negarse (a) to refuse (to)
negro black
nevar (ie) to snow
ni neither, nor; not even
    ni siquiera not even
nido nest
ninguno none
niño boy, child
no no; not
noche *(f.)* night
    de la noche al día overnight
    esta noche tonight
norte *(m.)* north
nota note; grade, mark
noticia news
novela novel
novia girlfriend
novio boyfriend
nuevo new
nunca never

• O •

o or
obligar to force

obra work
observar to observe
ocasión *(f.)* occasion
ocasionar to occasion
ocio idleness, leisure
ocupado occupied, busy
ocurrir to occur
ocho eight
odiar to hate
ofender to offend
oficina office
ofrecer to offer
oír to hear
ojalá I hope, I wish, if only
ojo eye
olvidar to forget
once eleven
operarse to be operated on, have an operation
oponer to oppose
    oponerse to object, be opposed
orden *(m.)* order; *(f.)* command
ordenar to order, arrange
orgulloso proud
oscuridad darkness
otro other, another
oveja sheep

• P •

padre father
    padres parents
pagar to pay
página page
país *(m.)* country; nation
paja straw
pájaro bird
palabra word
pan *(m.)* bread
pantalones *(m.)* pants
panzón fat-bellied
papa *(m.)* pope; *(f.)* potato
    ni papa nothing
papá father, dad

Papá Noel Santa Claus
papel *(m.)* paper
paquete *(m.)* package
par *(m.)* pair
para for; in order to
    para que in order that, so that
paradero whereabouts
paraguas *(m.)* umbrella
parecer to seem
pared *(f.)* wall
parte *(f.)* part
    por ninguna parte nowhere
    por todas partes everywhere
participar to participate
partido game, match
pasado past, last
pasajero passenger
pasar to pass, go by, come by; spend
    (time); happen
pasearse to walk (back and forth), stroll
paso step; pass, passage
pasta paste
pato duck
patria country; homeland
patrulla patrol
pedir (i) to ask for, request
pegar to hit
peinar to comb
película film
peligro danger
peligroso dangerous
pelo hair
pena grief
    pena de muerte capital punishment
    valer la pena to be worth the
    trouble
penoso painful
pensamiento thought
pensar (ie) to think; plan, intend
pequeño small
pera pear
percha hanger
perder (ie) to lose
pérdida loss
perdonar to forgive

perfeccionar to perfect
periódico newspaper
permitir to permit
pero but
persona person
pertenecer to belong
pertinente pertinent
perro dog
pesar to weigh
petizo pony
pianista pianist
picante hot, spicy
pie *(m.)* foot
    a pie on foot
    de pie standing up
pierna leg
pino pine
pío peeping
plaga plague
planeta *(m.)* planet
plantar to plant
platillo volante flying saucer
plato dish
    plato fuerte main course
pleno full
pliegue *(m.)* fold
plomo lead (metal)
pluma pen
pobre poor
poco little
poder to be able
poesía poetry; poem
polaco Polish
policía *(m.)* policeman; *(f.)* police force
política politics
polo pole
poner to put
    ponerse to put on; (sun) to go
    down
    ponerse a to begin
por for; per; by; through; during; on
    account of; for the sake of
    por eso that's why
    por favor please
    por fin finally

por lo menos at least
¿por qué? why?
por supuesto of course
porque because
portugués *(m.)* Portuguese
posible possible
posición position
practicar to practice
precio price
precioso precious; lovely
preciso necessary
predilecto favorite
preferir (ie) to prefer
pregunta question
preguntar to ask
   preguntarse to wonder
premio prize
preocuparse to worry
preparar to prepare
preparativo preparation
presencia presence
presentar to present
   presentarse to show up
presente present
presidente president
preso prisoner
prestar to loan, lend
   prestar atención to pay attention
presumir to presume, boast
primavera spring
primero first
primo cousin
principio beginning
prisa haste, hurry
privado private
probable probable
problema *(m.)* problem
profesor *(m.)* professor
programa *(m.)* program
prohibir to forbid
prometer to promise
pronto soon
propio own
proponer to propose
proteger to protect

proximidad proximity, nearness
próximo next
proyecto project
prueba proof; test
psiquiatra psychiatrist
publicar to publish
público audience
pueblo town; people
puerta door
pulcro clean, neat
punto point; period, dot
   en punto (time) sharp
puntual punctual

• Q •

que that; **¿qué?** what?
quedar to remain; be left
quejarse to complain
quemar to burn
querer to want; love
querido dear
queso cheese
quien who; **¿quién?** who?
quince fifteen
quinientos five hundred
quitar to remove
   quitarse to take off

• R •

rabia rage, fury; rabies
radicado located
rancho hut
rápido fast; quick
rato while
raza race (of people); breed
razón *(f.)* reason
   tener razón to be right
realidad reality
   en realidad actually
recibir to receive
   recibirse graduate

recitar to recite
recobrar to recover
recoger to pick up
recomendar (ie) to recommend
recordar (ue) to remember; remind
recorrido covering (of a distance)
referirse (ie) to refer
refrán *(m.)* proverb
regalar to give (as a present)
regalo gift, present
regreso return
reír (i) to laugh
religión *(f.)* religion
reloj *(m.)* watch, clock
remedio medicine; cure
renovar (ue) to renew
repente sudden movement or impulse
    de repente suddenly
repetir (i) to repeat
representar to represent
reprochar to reproach
requisito requirement
resolver (ue) to solve
respecto respect
respeto respect
    faltarle al respeto to be
    disrespectful to
responder to respond, reply
responsabilidad responsibility
responsable responsible
respuesta answer
resto rest
resultado result
resultar to turn out, result
retirar to take away
    retirarse to withdraw
retraso delay
reunión *(f.)* meeting
reunirse to meet
revista magazine
rico rich; tasty
ridículo ridiculous
rincón *(m.)* corner
río river
rodear to surround

rogar (ue) to beg
rojizo reddish
romano Roman
romper to break
ropa clothing
rosa rose
rosado pink
rotundo round; plain
rubio blond
ruborizarse to blush
rueda wheel
ruido noise
rumbo direction
    rumbo a in the direction of,
    heading for
Rusia Russia
ruso Russian
ruta route

• S •

saber to know
sabio wise; learned
sacar to take out; get (a grade);
    take (a picture)
saco coat
sagrado sacred
sala living room
    sala de espera waiting room
salida departure
salir to leave; go out, come out;
    turn out
salud *(f.)* health
salvaje wild
santo saint
sartén *(f.)* frying pan
satisfactorio satisfactory
satisfecho satisfied
secretario secretary
sed *(f.)* thirst
    tener sed to be thirsty
seda silk
seguida succession
    en seguida right away

seguir (i) to continue; follow
según according to (what)
segundo second
seguro sure; certain
seis six
semana week
semejante similar; such
semestre *(m.)* semester
sencillo simple
sensato sensible
sentar (ie) to seat
    sentarse to sit down
sentir (ie) to feel; to regret
señor gentleman
señora lady; wife
separar to separate
ser to be
    a no ser que unless
ser *(m.)* being
servicio service
servir (i) to serve
sí yes; indeed; **si** if
siempre always
    siempre que whenever
siete seven
siglo century
significar to mean
silla chair
simpático likable, nice, congenial
sin without
    sin embargo however
    un sin número many
sirvienta maid
sistema *(m.)* system
situación situation
sobre over, on
sobresaliente outstanding
sobrina niece
sobrino nephew
sobrio sober
sol *(m.)* sun
soler (ue) to be in the habit of
solo alone
sólo only
soltero single, unmarried

solución solution
sombrero hat
someter to subject
sonar (ue) to sound; ring
sonido sound
sonreír (i) to smile
soñar (ue) to dream
sopa soup
sorprender to surprise
sospechar to suspect
soya soybean
subir to go up, come up; get on
subjuntivo subjunctive
suceder to happen
sucio dirty
sueco Swedish
suela sole
sueño sleep; dream
sufrir to suffer
sugerencia suggestion
sugerir (ie) to suggest
sumamente extremely
suponer to suppose
surgir to arise, come up

• **T** •

tabla board, plank, table
tal such
    con tal que provided that
talla stature
tamaño size
también also
tan so
tanto so much, as much
    por lo tanto therefore
tardar to delay
tarde late; *(f.)* afternoon
tarjeta card
tarro jar, can
techo roof
teléfono telephone
televisión *(f.)* television
temer to fear

temor *(m.)* fear
temporada season
temprano early
tener to have
tercer(o) third
terminar to finish
término term
terremoto earthquake
testamento will
tía aunt
tiempo time; weather
tienda store
tierra land, earth
timbre *(m.)* bell
tinto (wine) red
tío uncle
tipo type; guy
tiránico tyrannical
títere *(m.)* puppet
tocadiscos *(m.)* record player
tocar to touch; (music) to play; to fall to
    one's lot, to be one's turn
todavía still, yet
todo all
tonto stupid
    hacerse el tonto to act dumb
toro bull
tostado toast
total *(m.)* total
trabajar to work
trabajo work, job
traducir to translate
traer to bring
traicionar to betray
traje *(m.)* suit
trampa trap; deception
    hacer trampas to cheat
tranquilidad tranquility
transcurrir to pass, elapse (time)
transporte *(m.)* transportation
trapo rag
tratar to treat
    tratar de to try to
trato agreement; care
travesura mischief, prank

tremendo terrible; huge
tren *(m.)* train
tres three
triste sad
turista tourist

• U •

últimamente lately
último last
único only; unique
universidad university
universitario *(adj.)* university
uno one
urdu Urdu
usar to use

• V •

vacío empty
vaquero cowboy
varios several
vecino neighbor
veinte twenty
vencer to win
vender to sell
venir to come
    la semana que viene next week
ventana window
ver to see
veracidad veracity
verano summer
veras truth, sincerity
    de veras really
verbo verb
verdad truth
verde green; unripe
verdura vegetable
versión *(f.)* version
vestido dress
vestidura clothing
vez *(f.)* occasion
    alguna vez ever

cada vez más more and more
de una vez once and for all
en vez de instead of
otra vez again
tal vez perhaps
una vez once
viaje *(m.)* trip
vicio vice; (bad) habit
vida life
viejo old
viento wind
viernes *(m.)* Friday
vietnamita Vietnamese
vino wine
visita visit; visitor
visitar to visit
vista sight; view
vivir to live
volante *(m.)* steering wheel
volver (ue) to return
volver a to . . . again
volverse to turn
voz *(f.)* voice
vuelta turn
dar vuelta to turn around

• Y •

y and
ya already; any more
ya no no longer, not any more
ya que since
yacer to lie
yerba mate mate tea

• Z •

zapatilla slipper
zapato shoe
zócalo town square

English/Spanish

Except for masculines ending in **-o (libro)** and feminines ending in **-a (casa)**, the gender of nouns is indicated by the appropriate definite article (**el papel, la carne**). Stem-changing verbs are indicated by **(ie)**, **(ue)**, or **(i)**.

List of Abbreviations

adj.	adjective	*m.*	masculine noun
adv.	adverb	*obj.*	object
conj.	conjunction	*prep.*	preposition
f.	feminine noun	*subj.*	subjunctive
inf.	infinitive	*v.*	verb

• A •

a(n) un, una (*See* Chapter 13)
ability la habilidad
about *(concerning)* sobre; acerca de
   about *(approximately)* unos . . . ;
   como . . .
accent acento
accept aceptar
accident el accidente
acclimate aclimatar
   to become acclimated aclimatarse
accompany acompañar
action la acción
actor actor
actress actriz

address *v.* dirigirse a
administrator administrador, -a
advise aconsejar
affection afecto
after *adv.* después; *prep.* después de;
   conj. después (de) que
afternoon la tarde
again otra vez
age la edad
ago hace (*See* Chapter 10)
agree (on) convenir (en)
airport aeropuerto
album el álbum
all todo

all over *(everywhere)* por todas partes
almost casi
alone solo
already ya
although aunque
always siempre
ambulance ambulancia
ancient antiguo;
   (referring to people) anciano
and y, *(before* i- *or* hi-*)* e
angry enojado
animal el animal
another otro
announce anunciar
answer *v.* contestar; *n.* respuesta
anybody alguien
   not . . . anybody nadie
anyone alguien
   not . . . anyone nadie
anything algo; cualquier cosa
   not . . . anything nada
anyway de cualquier modo; de todos modos
anywhere en cualquier parte
   not . . . anywhere en ninguna parte
apartment apartamento
appear aparecer
approach acercarse (a)
Argentine argentino
arise surgir
arrival llegada
arrive llegar
article artículo
ask *(inquire)* preguntar;
   (request, ask for) pedir (i)
assassinate asesinar
assume suponer
at en; a
atmosphere el ambiente; atmósfera
attack atacar
attend asistir a
attention la atención
   pay attention prestar atención
aunt tía

author autor, -a
authorize autorizar

• B •

back *(reverse side)* reverso
bad malo
   be too bad ser una lástima
badly mal
ball pelota
bare desnudo
barefoot descalzo
   go barefoot andar descalzo
barely apenas
bark ladrar
battle batalla
be ser; estar
   be able poder
   be about tratarse de
   be afraid tener miedo; temer
   be after querer
   be all gone haberse acabado
   be all right estar bien
   be back estar de vuelta
   be bored estar aburrido
   be cold *(referring to people)* tener frío; *(referring to the weather)* hacer frío
   be due to deberse a
   be glad estar contento; alegrarse (de)
   be hungry tener hambre
   be named llamarse
   be over estar terminado
   be quiet callarse
   be sorry sentir (ie)
   be worth valer
   be . . . years old tener . . . años
beautiful hermoso
beauty hermosura
because porque
become hacerse; ponerse
bed cama
before *adv.* antes; *prep.* antes de; *conj.* antes (de) que; *(in the presence of)* ante

begin empezar (ie); comenzar (ie);
   ponerse a
behave portarse (bien)
believe creer
belong pertenecer
beret boina
besides además (de)
best mejor
betray traicionar
better mejor
between entre
bicycle bicicleta
big grande
bill cuenta
birth nacimiento
birthday el cumpleaños
bite morder (ue)
black negro
blonde rubio
bloody sangriento
bloom florecer
blue azul
boat el bote
book libro
boring aburrido
boss el jefe, la jefa
bother molestar
   not to bother to no molestarse en
bottle botella
boxer boxeador, -a
boy muchacho; chico
bragging fanfarronería
branch rama
Brazil el Brasil
break romper
   break down descomponerse
breakfast desayuno
breeze brisa
bridge el puente
bring traer
brother hermano
building edificio
business negocio
   the business of lo de
but pero

buy comprar
by por; **by (play)ing** (jug)ando,
   by (sing)ing cantando, etc.

• C •

cafeteria cafetería
call llamar
can poder
capable capaz
capricious caprichoso
captain el capitán
capture capturar
car auto; el coche; carro
cardboard el cartón
care cuidado
   take care of cuidar
careful cuidadoso
   be careful tener cuidado
carefully con cuidado
carry llevar
   carry off llevarse
case caso
   in any case en cualquier caso
   just in case por si acaso
catch on comprender, entender
cause *v.* causar; *n.* causa
ceaseless constante
century siglo
chair silla
chamber cámara
   chamber of deputies cámara de
   diputados
change cambio
charge cargo
   in charge of a cargo de
charm encanto
Chilean chileno
Christmas Navidad
circle círculo
circular circular
circumstance circunstancia
city la ciudad
class la clase

clean limpiar
clear claro
close cerrar (ie)
coach entrenador, -a
coat chaqueta; saco; abrigo
coffee el café
cold frío
collect coleccionar
collection la colección
color el color
column columna
come venir
    come out salir
comfortable cómodo
communicate comunicar
company compañía
compare comparar
compete competir (i)
complete completar
completely completamente
concept concepto
concerning sobre
condition la condición
confess confesar (ie)
confidence confianza
conquest conquista
consent consentir
consequence consecuencia
consider considerar
constant constante
contemporary contemporáneo
continual continuo
continue continuar
contribution la contribución
convince convencer
cool enfriarse
copy copia
cordial cordial
corner esquina; el rincón
count contar (ue)
country el país
countryside el paisaje
courage el valor; el coraje
course curso
courteous cortés

cover cubrir
crazy loco
    drive crazy volver loco
credit crédito
cross atravesar
crush aplastar
curfew el toque de queda
cutting cortante

• D •

dad papá
damp húmedo
dance bailar
dare atreverse (a)
dark oscuro
darn maldito
daughter hija
dawn el amanecer
day el día
    day before yesterday anteayer
dead muerto
deal trato
dear querido
deceive engañar
decent decente
decide decidir
defend defender (ie)
doll muñeca
demand *v.* exigir; demandar
demise fallecimiento
dentist el/la dentista
deny negar (ie)
destination la destinación
detail el detalle
devil diablo
devilish endiablado
dictionary diccionario
die morir(se) (ue)
difference diferencia
different diferente
difficult difícil
dining room el comedor
dinner comida

dirty sucio
disappear desaparecer
discover descubrir
discrimination la discriminación
dish plato
display demostrar (ue)
distant lejano; distante
distinguished distinguido
do hacer
document documento
documentation la documentación
dog perro
dollar el dólar
door puerta
doubt *v.* dudar
draw dibujar
drink *v.* tomar; beber
drive *v. (referring to a vehicle)* manejar
driver el chofer; el conductor
    race-car driver el corredor de autos
drop dejar caer
    drop by . . . darse una vuelta por . . .
dry *v.* secar; *adj.* seco
due debido
dumb tonto
duration la duración
during durante

• E •

early temprano
earring el arete; el pendiente
earthquake terremoto
easy fácil
eat comer
education la educación
effort esfuerzo
else más
embarrass avergonzar (üe)
enchantment encanto
enclose encerrar (ie)
end el fin
energy energía
enjoy gozar

escapade escapada
escape escapar
essential esencial
eternity la eternidad
European europeo
evade evadir
even aun; hasta
    even if; even though aunque
    not even ni
ever alguna vez
    not . . . ever nunca
every todos los . . . ; cada
everybody todos
everything todo
everywhere en todas partes; por todas
    partes
exactly exactamente
exam el examen
exchange cambio
    in exchange for a cambio de
exercise ejercicio
exist existir
expect esperar
expensive caro
experience experiencia
explain explicar
explanation la explicación
express expresar
expression la expresión
eye ojo
eyelid párpado

• F •

face cara
fact el hecho
faded descolorido
fail fracasar
    fail to dejar de
faint *adj.* tenue
fall caer
    fall asleep dormirse (ue)
    fall down caerse
family familia

famous famoso
fantastic fantástico
far lejos
fast rápido
fatigue cansancio
favorite favorito
feel sentir (ie) + *noun*; sentirse (ie) + *adj.*
　　or adv.
　　feel bad sentirse mal
feverish febril
few pocos
　　a few unos pocos
fifth quinto
fight pelear; luchar
figure figura
fill llenar
film película
find encontrar (ue); hallar
　　find out enterarse (de); saber
finish terminar; acabar
fireplace el hogar; chimenea
first primero
　　at first al principio
fish pescado
five cinco
fix arreglar; componer
floor suelo; piso
flower la flor
food comida
foot el pie; *(of an animal)* pata
　　put one's foot in it meter la pata
for por; para (*See* Chapter 18)
forbid prohibir
force *v.* obligar; forzar
forehead la frente
forget olvidarse (de)
forgive perdonar
fortunate afortunado
fortune fortuna
four cuatro
frank franco
free librar
freedom la libertad
fresh fresco
fresh-cut recién cortado

friend amigo
from de
front el frente
　　in front of delante de
fry freir (i)
full lleno
furious furioso
furtive furtivo
future futuro

• G •

game juego; *(match)* partido
garden el jardín
gasoline gasolina
generation la generación
generally generalmente
gentleman señor
German alemán, -ana
get conseguir; *(become)* hacerse;
　　ponerse
　　get away escapar(se)
　　get here llegar
　　get in entrar; pasar
　　get in touch with ponerse en
　　contacto con
　　get involved in meterse en
　　get mad enojarse
　　get out salir
　　get sick enfermarse
　　get to llegar a
　　get to work ponerse a trabajar
　　get up levantarse
gigantic gigantesco
girl muchacha, chica
give dar; *(give a gift)* regalar
　　give back devolver (ue)
glasses los lentes
　　dark glasses lentes ahumados
glitter relucir
glove el guante
go ir
　　go back volver (ue)
　　go by pasar

go out salir
go to bed acostarse (ue)
go to sleep dormirse (ue)
go up subir
gold oro
good n. el bien; adj. bueno
for good para siempre
good and . . . bien . . .
government gobierno
grass pasto; hierba
gray gris
grayish grisáceo
great grande
green verde
greenish-blue verdeazul
group grupo
guard el/la guarda
guerrilla guerrillero
guitar guitarra
guy tipo

• H •

hair cabello; pelo
half medio
hand la mano
handmade hecho a mano
handsome guapo
hang colgar (ue)
be hanging on (referring to words, news, etc.) estar pendiente de
happen ocurrir; suceder
happy contento; feliz
hard duro; (difficult) difícil
hardly apenas
hardly ever casi nunca
hate odiar
have tener
have to tener que
have left quedarle a uno
he él
headache el dolor de cabeza
hear oír
heaven cielo

for heaven's sake por Dios
heavy pesado
height estatura; altura
help ayudar
not to be able to help it no poder más
help ayuda
her obj. of verb la, le; obj. of prep. ella (See Chapter 11)
here aquí
around here por aquí
hers su(s) (See Chapter 16)
herself obj. of verb se; obj. of prep. sí (See Chapter 12)
him obj. of verb lo, le; obj. of prep. él (See Chapter 11)
himself obj. of verb se; obj. of prep. sí (See Chapter 12)
his su(s) (See Chapter 16)
hit v. pegar
home casa
at home en casa
homeland patria
hope v. esperar; n. esperanza
horizon el horizonte
horse caballo
hospital el hospital
hot caliente
hotel el hotel
hour hora
house casa
how? ¿cómo?
humid húmedo
hurry prisa
in a hurry con prisa
hurt lastimar; doler

• I •

I yo
if si
as if como si
ignore no hacer caso (de)
illustrious ilustre

imagine imaginar(se)
importance importancia
important importante
impose imponer
impossible imposible
impress impresionar
impression la impresión
in en
incessant incesante
incident el incidente
inconsequential de poca importancia
incredible increíble
indicate indicar
indispensable indispensable
infinite infinito
influence *v.* influir (en); *n.* influencia
information la información
injustice injusticia
innocent inocente
insist (on) insistir (en)
inspiring inspirador
insult insultar
intelligent inteligente
intention la intención
interfere interponerse
interview entrevista
intimate íntimo
introduce presentar
ironic irónico
irregular irregular
isolated aislado
it *obj. of verb* lo, la, le; *obj. of prep.* él,
    ella, (*See* Chapter 11)
Italy Italia
itself se (*See* Chapter 12)

• J •

Japan el Japón
job puesto
joke el chiste
jump saltar
June junio
junk basura
just *(only)* solamente

• K •

keep guardar
key la llave
kid chico
kidnap secuestrar
kill matar
know saber; conocer
    know how to saber

• L •

lady señora
landscape el paisaje
last último
    the last of *(a month, year, etc.)*
    fines de
late tarde
    get late hacerse tarde
Latin American latinoamericano
laugh reírse (i)
lawyer abogado
lead dirigir
    lead a . . . life llevar una vida · · ·
leader líder
leafy frondoso
league liga
learn aprender
least menor; menos
    at least por lo menos
leave salir, irse
left izquierdo
    on the left a la izquierda
legal legal
lend prestar
lesson la lección
let dejar, permitir
letter carta
lie *v.* mentir (ie); *n.* mentira
life vida
light la luz
like *v.* gustarle a uno; *(referring to liking*
    people) caerle bien
like *adv. and prep.* como

likely probable
literature literatura
live vivir
located situado
long largo
    as long as mientras
    how long cuánto tiempo
longer más tiempo
    not . . . any longer ya no, no . . . más
look *(seem) v.* parecer; *n.* mirada
    look at mirar
    look for buscar
    look like parecerse a
lord señor
    good Lord! ¡Dios mío!
lose perder (ie)
lot el lote
    a lot mucho
loud fuerte
love *v.* amar; querer; *n.* el amor

• M •

mad enojado
mainly principalmente
make hacer
man el hombre
manage (to) alcanzar (a); poder
mane melena
manuscript manuscrito
many muchos
    how many? ¿cuántos?
    so many tantos
map el mapa
matter *v.* importar; *n.* asunto
    no matter how . . . por . . . que
    + *subj.* (*por bien que cante,* etc.)
    no matter what . . . *subj.* + lo que
    + *subj.* (*digan lo que digan,* etc.)
maybe tal vez
me *obj. of verb* me; *obj. of prep.* mí
    (*See* Chapter 11)
means medio

by no means de ninguna manera
measure *v.* medir (i); *n.* medida
meat la carne
meddle (in) meterse (en)
medicine medicina
medium mediano
meet encontrar (ue); *(make the
    acquaintance of)* conocer
meeting la reunión
memory recuerdo; memoria
mention mencionar
Mexico City (la ciudad de) México
mile milla
millionaire millonario
mind la mente
    slip one's mind olvidársele a uno
minute minuto
mistaken equivocado
mix *v.* mezclar
modern moderno
moment momento
momentary momentáneo
money dinero
month el mes
    next month el mes que viene
more más
    more than más de
    not any more ya no
morning *n.* mañana; *adj.* matinal
most más
mother la madre
mountain montaña
mouth boca
move *(change residence)* mudarse
movement movimiento
much mucho
    how much? ¿cuánto?
    so much tanto
multicolored multicolor
multitude la multitud
murderer asesino
musty mohoso
must deber, tener que
myself *obj. of verb* me; *obj. of prep.* mí
    (*See* Chapter 12)

• N •

narrow angosto; estrecho
near cerca (de)
necessary necesario
necklace el collar
need *v.* necesitar; hacerle falta a uno;
    n. la necesidad
neighbor vecino
neighborhood barrio; la vecindad
never nunca
nevertheless sin embargo
new nuevo
news noticia
next próximo
night la noche
    last night anoche
nine nueve
no no
nobody nadie
none ninguno
northerly norteño
not no
novel novela
now ahora
nowadays hoy en día
New York Nueva York
nuclear nuclear
nuisance molestia
nut *(referring to a person)* chiflado

• O •

obligation la obligación
obtain obtener
obvious obvio
obviously obviamente
occasion la ocasión
occur ocurrir
of de
offend ofender
offer *v.* ofrecer
official oficial
old viejo

on en
once una vez (que)
one uno
only *adv.* sólo; solamente; *adj.* único
open *v.* abrir
opinion la opinión
opportunity la oportunidad
oppose oponer
    be opposed to oponerse a
or o, *(before* o- *or* ho-*)* u
order pedir (i)
order el orden; *(command)* la orden;
    (commercial) pedido
    in order to para
    in order that para que
other otro
otherwise si no, de otra manera
ought deber
ourselves *obj. of verb* nos; *obj. of prep.*
    nosotros *(See* Chapter 12)
out fuera
overcoat abrigo; sobretodo
overlook pasar por alto

• P •

package el paquete
painful doloroso
paint pintar
painting pintura
pair el par
pants los pantalones
paper el papel
paragraph párrafo
park el parque
part la parte
    on the part of de parte de
participate participar
party fiesta
pass *v.* pasar
past pasado
paste pegar
patience paciencia
patriot el/la patriota

pay pagar
peaceful pacífico
pedantic pedante
pen pluma
penetrate penetrar
people la gente
perfectly perfectamente
performance la función; la actuación
period período; época
permission permiso
permit permitir
perseverance perseverancia
person persona
pick up recoger
picture cuadro; *(portrait)* retrato
piece pedazo; trozo
place colocar
place el lugar
plan *v.* proyectar
   plan to pensar (ie)
play *(a game)* jugar (ue); *(music)* tocar
player jugador
   soccer player futbolista; jugador(a)
   de fútbol
please por favor
pleased contento
poem poesía
politician político
poor pobre
pork cerdo
Portuguese portugués
position la posición
possible posible
   as . . . as possible lo más . . .
   posible
postpone postergar
prefer preferir (ie)
preference preferencia
prepare preparar
present presentar
present *n.* el presente; *(gift)* regalo
   adj. presente
presidente el/la presidente
prevent impedir (i)
previous anterior

price precio
prize premio
problem el problema
proceed proceder
professor profesor, -a
project proyecto
promise prometer
protect proteger
protest protestar
provided that con tal que
purpose propósito
purse bolsa
put poner; colocar; meter
   put away guardar
   put on ponerse
   put to bed acostar (ue)

• Q •

question pregunta
   ask a question hacer una pregunta
quick rápido

• R •

race carrera
racial racial
rag trapo
rain *v.* llover (ue); *n.* lluvia
rapid rápido
rather bastante
read leer
ready listo
realize darse cuenta (de)
reason la razón
receive recibir
receptionist recepcionista
recite recitar
recognize reconocer

recommend recomendar (ie)
record disco
recovery la recuperación
redhead pelirrojo
refuse *v.* negarse (a)
regards recuerdos
region la región
regret sentir (ie)
relax calmarse
remains restos
remember acordarse (ue) (de);
   recordar (ue)
remind (of) recordar
remorse remordimiento
rent alquilar
repeat repetir (i)
repent arrepentirse (ie)
request rogar (ue)
rescue el rescate
respect *v.* respetar; *n.* respeto
responsible responsable
rest descansar
restaurant el restaurante; el restorán
result resultado
return *(go back)* volver (ue); *(give back)*
   devolver (ue)
revolutionary revolucionario
ride andar
ridiculous ridículo
right bien
   right away en seguida
right derecho
   on the right a la derecha
ring anillo
rock roca, piedra
role el papel
   play a role hacer un papel
romantic romántico
roof techo
room cuarto
round redondo
rule *n.* regla
run correr; marchar
   take off running salir corriendo
rustic rústico

• S •

sad triste
same mismo
satisfied satisfecho
save salvar; ahorrar
say decir
   say good-bye (to) despedirse (i) (de)
   say hello (to) saludar
scandalize escandalizar
scene escena
school escuela
scold reñir
search buscar
   in search of en busca de
seat asiento
section la sección
see ver
seek buscar
seem parecer
sell vender
send enviar; mandar
separate separar
serve servir (i)
session la sesión
seven siete
shake sacudir
shape forma
share compartir
sheet *(referring to paper)* hoja
shelter amparar; proteger
shirt camisa
shoe zapato
short corto; breve
short story cuento
shoulder hombro
shout gritar
show mostrar (ue); enseñar
   show up aparecer; presentarse
shower *v.* ducharse; *n.* ducha
side lado
sidewalk acera
sight vista
sign el cartel; letrero

significance significado
silhouette silueta
simply simplemente
since *(time)* desde (que); *(cause)* ya que, puesto que
sing cantar
sir señor
sit down sentarse (ie)
sleep dormir (ue)
slip *n.* descuido
slow lento
small pequeño
smart listo
smile sonreír (i)
smile sonrisa
smooth liso
snow *v.* nevar (ie); *n.* la nieve
so así; **so** + *adj. or adv.* tan
soccer el fútbol
social social
soft suave
solution la solución
somebody alguien
someone alguien
something algo
    something of the sort algo por el estilo
sometimes a veces
somewhat algo
somewhere en alguna parte
song la canción
soon pronto
    as soon as tan pronto como; en cuanto
Spain España
Spanish *n.* español; *adj.* español, -a
spark chispa; chispazo
speak hablar
specific específico
speech discurso
speedy rápido
spend (time) pasar
spit escupir
spite despecho
    in spite of a pesar de

sport el deporte
spread *(propagate)* propagar
spring primavera
stand *(endure)* aguantar
    stand up ponerse de pie; pararse
start *v.* empezar (ie); comenzar (ie)
state estado
stay quedarse
step *n.* paso
stick pegar
still *adj.* quieto; *adv.* todavía
stop parar; detenerse
    stop . . . -ing dejar de + *inf.*
store *n.* tienda
storm tormenta
story cuento
stream arroyo
street la calle
stripe franja
stroll *v.* pasearse
strong fuerte
student *n.* el/la estudiante; *adj.* estudiantil
study estudiar
stupid estúpido
subject materia
succeed (in) lograr
such (a) tal
suddenly de repente
suffer sufrir
suggest sugerir (ie)
suitcase maleta
sun el sol
support *v.* apoyar; *n.* apoyo
suppose suponer
sure seguro
    for sure con seguridad
surprise sorpresa
surprising sorprendente
survive sobrevivir
swear jurar
sweater el suéter
sweet dulce

• T •

table mesa
take tomar; llevar; aguantar
    take a step backward dar un paso para atrás
    take command of asumir el mando de
    take off *(remove)* quitar
talk *v.* hablar; *(converse)* charlar; *n.* charla
tall alto
Tangier Tánger
tape *n.* cinta
taste saber; probar (ue)
teacher maestro; profesor, -a
tear romper
tear lágrima
telegram el telegrama
tell decir; contar (ue)
ten diez
tenth décimo
term término
terrible terrible
terribly tremendamente
test el examen
textbook libro de texto
than *(comparing two persons or things)* que; *(comparing two amounts or quantities)* del que (de la que, de los que, de las que, de lo que) (*See* Chapter 14)
that ese; aquel (*See* Chapter 16); que
the el, la, los, las (*See* Chapter 13)
them *obj. of verb* los, las, les; *obj. of prep.* ellos (-as) (*See* Chapter 11)
theme el tema
themselves *obj. of verb* se; *obj. of prep.* sí (*See* Chapter 12)
then entonces
there allí
    around there por allí
there to be haber
there is, there are hay

they ellos (-as)
thick grueso, espeso
thief el ladrón
thing cosa
think pensar (ie); creer
    think about pensar en
third tercer
though aunque
thousand mil
three tres
throw (out) tirar
ticket boleto
tie corbata
till hasta (que)
time tiempo; *(occasion)* la vez; *(time of day)* hora
    at that time en ese entonces
    at the same time a la misma vez
    by this time para ahora
    have a good time divertirse (ie)
    on time a tiempo; a hora
timid tímido
tired cansado
to a
today hoy
tolerate tolerar
tomorrow mañana
tonight esta noche
too demasiado
top la parte superior
    in (at) the top en lo alto
torrential torrencial
tourist el/la turista
tournament campeonato
toward hacia, para
tower la torre
town pueblo
track huella
tragic trágico
train el tren
tree el árbol
trembling tembloroso
tremendous tremendo
trouble preocupar
trouble el problema

to be in trouble tener problema
truck el camión
true verdadero
   be true ser verdad
trust *v.* confiar (en)
truth la verdad
try tratar (de); *(sample)* probar (ue)
Tuesday mártes
turn in entregar
   turn out resultar
turn turno
twenty veinte
two dos
type tipo

• U •

ugly feo
umbrella el paraguas
unbearable intolerable; insoportable
uncle tío
uncomfortable incómodo
under bajo
understand entender (ie); comprender
uniquely singularmente
unimaginable inimaginable
unless a menos que
unnoticed desapercibido
until hasta (que)
up arriba
   up to hasta
us *obj. of verb* nos; *obj. of prep.*
   nosotros (-as) *(See* Chapter 11)
use usar

• V •

vacation las vacaciones
vague vago
verb verbo
very muy
visit visitar

• W •

wait (for) esperar
walk *v.* caminar
wall la pared
want *v.* querer
war guerra
warmth el calor
warn advertir (ie)
wash *v.* lavar
watch *v.* mirar; ver
watch *n.* el reloj
way manera; modo
   that way así
we nosotros (-as)
wear llevar
weather tiempo
Wednesday miércoles
week semana
   last week la semana pasada
well bien
well-known conocido
what? ¿qué?; lo que *(See* Chapter 17)
wheel rueda
   steering wheel el volante
when cuando
whenever siempre que
where donde
whereabouts paradero
which que, el que, el cual *(See*
   Chapter 17)
while mientras
white blanco
who que, quien *(See* Chapter 17)
whole todo
wholesale al por mayor
why? ¿por qué?
wild silvestre
willing (to) dispuesto (a)
win ganar
wind viento
window ventana
wine vino
winter invierno
wipe out borrar

wire el alambre, el cable
wish *v.* desear; *n.* deseo
    I wish *(if only)* ojalá (que)
witchcraft brujería
with con
withdraw retirarse
without sin (que)
woman la mujer
wonder *v.* preguntarse
wool lana
word palabra
work *v.* trabajar; *n.* trabajo; *(literary or artistic work)* obra
worry preocuparse
write escribir
writer escritor
writing escritura
    in writing por escrito
wrong equivocado

• Y •

year año
yell gritar
yellow amarillo
yesterday ayer
yet todavía
yield rendir (i); ceder
you *subj.* tú, vosotros (-as), usted(es); *obj. of verb* te, os, lo(s), la(s), le(s) (*See* Chapter 11); *obj. of prep.* ti, vosotros (-as), usted(es); *(one)* se (*See* Chapter 12)
young joven
your tu(s), vuestro (-a, -os, -as), su(s) (*See* Chapter 16)
yourself *obj. of verb* te, se; *obj. of prep.* ti, sí (*See* Chapter 12)

Index